SCIENCE AND RELIGION

SCIENCE AND RELIGION

Swami Ranganathananda

Advaita Ashrama
(Publication Department)
5 Dehi Entally Road
Kolkata 700 014

Published by
Swami Bodhasarananda
President, Advaita Ashrama
Mayavati, Champawat, Uttarakhand
from its Publication Department, Kolkata
Email: mail@advaitaashrama.org
Website: www.advaitaashrama.org

First Edition, June 1978
Tenth Impression, May 2007
3M3C

ISBN 81-7505-035-7

Printed in India at
Trio Process
Kolkata 700 014

PREFACE

In response to the invitation of the Bangalore University to inaugurate its seventeen-lecture-series programme on *Science, Society, and the Scientific Attitude,* Swami Ranganathananda addressed a meeting on 'Science and Religion' at the Senate Hall of the University on 5 August 1976. The University later published that lecture as a book, for presentation to the graduates of the University at its annual Convocation.

In view of the topical importance of the subject, and with a view to reaching a wider reading public in India and abroad, we are happy to bring out this edition of the lecture in book form, after suitable revision by the Swami. Another lecture on *'Faith and Reason'*, delivered by the Swami at the Ramakrishna Ashrama, Gwalior, on 26 May 1976, and revised by him, has also been included in this book, being closely relevant to the main theme.

We wish to offer our sincere thanks to Swami Kirtidananda, Secretary, Ramakrishna Mission Students' Home, Madras-600004, for preparing the Index to this book in the midst of his onerous duties of the Home.

Advaita Ashrama
Mayavati, Himalayas
15 June 1978

PUBLISHER

CONTENTS

I. SCIENCE AND RELIGION

KEY TO TRANSLITERATION AND PRONUNCIATION

a	अ	*Sounds like*	o in s*o*n
ā	आ	,,	a in m*a*ster
i	इ	,,	i in *i*f
ī	ई	,,	ee in f*ee*l
u	उ	,,	u in f*u*ll
ū	ऊ	,,	oo in b*oo*t
ṛ	ऋ	,,	somewhat between r and ri
e	ए	,,	a in ev*a*de
ai	ऐ	,,	y in m*y*
o	ओ	,,	o in *o*ver
au	औ	,,	ow in n*ow*
k	क	,,	k
kh	ख	,,	ckh in blo*ckh*ead
g	ग	,,	g (hard)
gh	घ	,,	gh in lo*g-h*ut
ṅ	ङ	,,	ng
c	च	,,	ch (not k)
ch	छ	,,	chh in cat*ch h*im
j	ज	,,	j
jh	झ	,,	dgeh in he*dgeh*og
ñ	ञ	,,	n (somewhat)
ṭ	ट	,,	t
ṭh	ठ	,,	th in an*t-h*ill

ḍ	ड	,,	d
ḍh	ढ	,,	dh in godhood
ṇ	ण	,,	n in under
t	त	,,	t in (French
th	थ	,,	th in thumb
d	द	,,	th in then
dh	ध	,,	theh in breathe here
n	न	,,	n
p	प	,,	p
ph	फ	,,	ph in loop-hole
b	ब	,,	b
bh	भ	,,	bh in abhor
m	म	,,	m
y	य	,,	y
r	र	,,	r
l	ळ	,,	l
v	व	,,	v in avert
ś	श	,,	sh
ṣ	ष	,,	sh in show
s	स	,,	s
h	ह	,,	h
ṁ	·	,,	m in mum
ḥ	ह	,,	h in huh !

Lecture I

SCIENCE AND RELIGION*

1. *Introduction*

I am thankful to the Bangalore University and its Vice-Chancellor, Dr. H. Narasimhaiah, for the invitation extended to me to speak on *Science and Religion* at this first inaugural session of its lecture series on *Science, Society, and the Scientific Attitude.*

2. *Need to Foster the Scientific Spirit*

Modern environmental and ecological problems may be making for the unpopularity of technology, or rather of over-technology, especially in advanced countries ; but *pure science, with its passion for truth and human welfare, will always remain as one of the noblest pursuits of man ;*

---

* First lecture, under the auspices of the Bangalore University, on 5 August 1976, in its 17-themes lecture

and our country, which has nurtured this love and pursuit of truth in the fields of physical sciences, religion, and philosophy in the past, must continue to nurture it in all fields in the modern age. Religion and philosophy in India, as given to us in our Upaniṣadic tradition, is but the continuation of the scientific search for truth at the sense-data level to the higher aesthetic, ethical, and spiritual levels of experience, as I hope to show in the course of this address. I appreciate this pioneer effort of the Bangalore University to inculcate the scientific spirit among its students and staff and the general citizens. *I wish, however, that the training of our people in the scientific attitude and outlook begins from the stage of primary education itself.* That is the only way to purify and strengthen the rational and spiritual heritage of our country by draining away its impure, weakening, and centuries-old contaminations of magic and superstition.

3. Relationship of Science and Religion: A New Approach

The subjects of science and religion are getting more and more important to man in the modern

---

series on *Science, Society, and the Scientific Attitude*; a revised version of the original lecture.

age. They are two great disciplines which, in the light of Indian wisdom, reveal that, when relied on separately, can be counter-productive in the long run, but, when combined harmoniously, can bring about an all-round expression of human genius and total fulfilment. But, unfortunately, for the last few centuries, the relationship between the two in the Western context, and everywhere else also due to the world-wide impact of Western culture, has not been quite happy. In the twentieth century, however, a new approach is becoming evident, and the representative thinkers among scientists and religious people are beginning to discern a close interrelation between them. They are slowly veering round to the point of view that science and religion can heartily embrace each other, without detriment to the cause for which each stands, and work for the good of humanity. It is being realised more and more by both that there are elements in science that religion can adopt in order to fortify itself, and elements in religion that can deepen and strengthen science. I shall here touch upon some of the sources of the discord between the two and the significance of the points of contract between them, and discuss the methods and results of both the disciplines, *against the background, and in the light, of the unity and totality of all human knowledge and the synthetic and synoptic approach and vision of the Indian philosophical and spiritual tradition.*

4. *The Scientific Discipline*

The civilisation in which we live today is the product of the discipline of the human mind known as modern science. When we study science at close quarters, in the way the great scientists have applied themselves to this pursuit, we find two aspects to this discipline. The first is *pure science,* science which tries earnestly to understand the truth of nature through a dispassionate inquiry ; and the second is *applied science,* in which the truth discovered by pure science flows as technical inventions for the enhancement and enrichment of human life. These two, science as *lucifera* and science as *fructifera,* science as *light* and science as *fruit,* are intimately related. Knowledge leads to power and power leads to control and manipulation of the forces of nature, enabling man to condition his life and environment with deliberation. Every new discovery in pure science, at some stage or other, becomes converted into applied science, into control and manipulation of the forces of nature. And the result, as revealed in recent history, is the great saga of modern scientific discovery and invention resulting in the world-wide technological civilisation of today. It is a most fascinating study how the human mind, disciplined in this pursuit of science, develops the capacity to wrest from nature truth after truth, hidden and jealously guarded by her, leading to our extraordinary modern age of nuclear science and space travel.

What is the nature of that movement of thought which has produced these remarkable results? What do we mean by the term 'modern' as applied to thought, and what is the special feature of modern scientific thought which has rendered thought so explosive and revolutionary? An answer to these questions will help us to reassess the role of the other great human disciplines, such as religion, ethics, art, politics, and economics in the modern age.

The architect of the modern world is science, and by modern thought is meant scientific thought. The aim of science is to study nature and human experience objectively. To quote Karl Pearson (*Grammar of Science,* 1900, p. 6):

> 'The classification of facts, the recognition of their sequence and relative significance, is the function of science, and the habit of forming a judgement upon these facts unbiased by personal feeling is characteristic of what may be termed the scientific frame of mind.'

This quality of the scientific mind, and the mood and temper of its approach, have enabled science to wrest from nature its secrets, first from one field, then from another, and transform nature's forces into agencies for the service of man. The sum total of achievements in the theoretical and practical fields in the various departments of scientific inquiry in physics and chemistry, mathematics and astronomy, biology and psychology, as also in their various subsidiary branches, constitute an impressive record of human development, by the side of which long ages of past achievements in the same fields pale into insignificance. That is modern science in its methods and results.

5. *Science versus Departments of Science*

Science so understood is not tied up with any particular body of facts. In the words of one of the great biologists, J. Arthur Thomson (*Introduction to Science,* Home University Library edition, p. 58) :

'Science is not wrapped up with any particular body of facts; it is characterised as an intellectual attitude. It is not tied down to any particular methods of inquiry; it is simple sincere critical thought, which admits conclusions only when these are based on evidence. *We may get a good lesson in scientific method from a businessman meeting some new practical problem, from a lawyer sifting evidence, or from a statesman framing a constructive bill.*' (italics not by the author).

Objectivity and precision, both as to thought and its verbal formulation, are two important characteristics of the scientific method. Any study possessing these characteristics will be science, whatever be the field of that study. Science as such is, therefore, not tied down to any particular order of facts, though the various departments of science, like physics or chemistry, biology or sociology, are tied down to particular orders of facts. These departments have limited scope, but science itself is unlimited in scope ; and these various departments, starting with the study of separate fields tend, in their advanced stages, to overstep their particular boundaries and merge into one converging scientific search, the search for the meaning of total experience. *In this expansive context, the idea of a science of religion, the science of the facts of the inner world of man, as upheld in ancient Indian thought, and as expounded in the modern age by Swami Vivekananda, becomes also a scientific study of far-reaching significance.*

6. *The Spirit of Inquiry*

The driving force behind this unique modern achievement is the spirit of free inquiry characteristic of modern science. The mind that questions, and questions with a serious intent and purpose, and tests and verifies the answers it gets, has a dynamic quality about it, which enables it to forge ahead in the world of thought and things. In so forging ahead, it disturbs the wayside calm of untested dogmas and comfortable beliefs, and the magic and miracle and superstition wrongly associated with religion and leading to the vulgarisation of this great discipline. Science is verified knowledge. The explosive character of modern scientific thought is the product of the impact of a rapid succession of verified knowledge against an intractable fund of untested dogmas, assumptions, beliefs, magic, miracle, and superstitions. The organised opposition of the latter in the West sought to stifle scientific inquiry, first, at its birth and, later, at every stage of its progress. But the walls of the *bastille* of ignorance and prejudice fell one by one before the onrushing waves of inquiry and illumination, illustrating the great saying of the Upaniṣads (*Muṇḍaka Upaniṣad*, III, 1.6) :

'*Satyameva jayate, nānṛtam*—Truth alone triumphs, not untruth.'

The history of science in recent centuries is thus the history of the triumph of the spirit of free inquiry over mere opinion, untested belief, prejudice and dogma. It is a remarkable adventure of the human spirit which has borne abundant fruits, not only mental but also material; for science as *lucifera* has flowed into science as *fructifera,* giving a bumper crop of discoveries and inventions which has transformed beyond recognition the world in which we live.

7. *Eclipse of Dogma-bound Religion*

The success of science has meant the defeat of its opponent. It is one of the unfortunate episodes of history, especially of modern European history, that the organisation of the forces of prejudice and blind belief against science and its spirit of inquiry came from the side of religion ; and that, reason, which is the life-breath of science, was viewed as the death-knell of religion. By the end of the last century, science had acquired high prestige and authority, while religion had been discredited, first, as a dangerous error, and later, as a harmless illusion.

The end of the nineteenth century thus saw the eclipse of religion in the West. But there was an uneasy feeling in the hearts of many thinkers that something of deep value to man and his civilisation had been overthrown ; and they attempted a reassessment of the meaning and scope of religion with a view to making it accord with the spirit and temper of science. *To this great task of reconstructing the mental life of modern man by bridging the gulf between faith and reason, on the basis of a unified view of man and a truer conception of the spiritual life, the contribution of Indian thought is unique and lasting.*

8. Vivekananda on Reason and Religion

Tracing the recurring conflicts of science and religion in the West to the absence of a broad rational and experiential approach, Vivekananda said (*Complete Works,* Vol. II, ninth edition, p. 433) :

'We all know the theories of the cosmos according to the modern astronomers and physicists, and at the same time we all know how woefully they undermine the theology of Europe ; how these scientific discoveries that are made act as a bomb thrown at its stronghold ; and we know how theologians have in all times attempted to put down these researches.'

When religion refuses to take the help of reason, it weakens itself. Alluding to this in the course of a lecture on 'Reason and Religion', delivered in England in 1896, Swami Vivekananda said (*ibid.*, Vol. I, eleventh edition, p. 367) :

'The foundations have been all undermined, and the modern man, whatever he may say in public, knows in the privacy of his heart that he can no more "believe". Believing certain things because an organised body of priests tells him to believe, believing because it is written in certain books, believing because his people like him to believe, the modern man knows to be impossible for him. There are, of course, a number of people who seem to acquiesce in the so-called popular faith, but we also know for certain that they do not think. Their idea of belief may be better translated as "not-thinking-carelessness".'

And pleading for the application of reason in the field of religion, he continued (*ibid.*) :

'Is religion to justify itself by the discoveries of reason through which every other science justifies itself ? Are the same methods of investigation, which we apply to science and knowledge outside, to be applied to the science of religion ? In my opinion, this must be so ; and I am also of opinion that the sooner it is done the better. If a religion is destroyed by such investigations, it was then all the time useless, unworthy, superstition ;

and the sooner it goes the better. I am thoroughly convinced that its destruction would be the best thing that could happen. All that is dross will be taken off, no doubt, but the essential parts of religion will emerge triumphant out of this investigation. Not only will it be made scientific—as scientific, at least, as any of the conclusions of physics or chemistry—but it will have greater strength, because physics or chemistry has no internal mandate to vouch for its truth which religion has.'

A study of the Upaniṣads reveals that the subject of religion was approached in ancient India in an objective dispassionate manner; and the aim of the study was to get at truth, and not to hug pleasing fancies and illusions or to idolise tribal passions and prejudices.

In several of his lectures and discourses, Swami Vivekananda has expounded this scientific approach as upheld in Indian thought. In his lecture on 'Religion and Science', he says (*ibid.*, Vol. VI sixth edition, p. 81):

'Experience is the only source of knowledge. In the world, religion is the only science where there is no surety, because it is not taught as a science of experience. This should not be. There is always, however, a small group of men who teach religion from experience. They are called mystics, and these mystics in every religion speak the same tongue and teach the same truth. This is the real science of religion. As mathematics in every part of the world does not differ, so the mystics do not differ. They are all similarly constituted and similarly situated. Their experience is the same; and this becomes law. . . .

'Religion deals with the truths of the metaphysical world, just as chemistry and the other natural sciences deal with the truths of the physical world. The book one must read to learn chemistry is the book of nature. The book from which to learn religion is your own mind and heart. The sage is often ignorant of physical science, because he reads the wrong book—the book within; and the scientist is too often ignorant of religion, because he, too, reads the wrong book—the book without.'

The Indian thinkers discovered by their investigations that there are two fields in which man lives and functions; one, the external world; the other, the internal. These are two different orders of phenomena. The study of the one alone does not exhaust the whole range of experience. Also, the study of the one from the standpoint of the other will not lead to satisfactory results. But the study of the one *in the light of the conclusions from the study of the other* is helpful and relevant.

Referring to this approach in the course of a lecture on 'Cosmology', Swami Vivekananda said (*ibid.*, Vol. II, ninth edition, p. 432):

'There are two worlds, the microcosm and the macrocosm, the internal and the external. We get truth from both of these by means of experience. The truth gathered from internal experience is psychology, metaphysics, and religion ; from external experience, the physical sciences. Now, a perfect truth should be in harmony with experiences in both these worlds. The microcosm must bear testimony to the macrocosm, and the macrocosm to the microcosm ; physical truth must have its counterpart in the internal world, and the internal world must have its verification outside.'

Thus the sages and thinkers of ancient India said : Here is the physical life of man, and here is the physical universe that environs him. Let us study both in a scientific spirit. But let us also study him in his depths, his nature as revealed by his consciousness, his thoughts, his emotions, his ego, and his sense of selfhood. These latter also constitute a vast group of phenomena that need to be investigated. Every advance in this field is bound to advance man's knowledge about the truth of the mystery of the external world. For, to quote mathematician-astronomer, the late Sir Arthur Eddington (*Philosophy of Physical Science,* p. 5):

'We have discovered that it is actually an aid in the search for knowledge to understand the nature of the knowledge which we seek.'

9. *The Upaniṣads and the Spirit of Critical Inquiry in India*

Ever since the time of the Upaniṣads, India has tenaciously held to a view of religion which makes it a high adventure of the spirit, a converging life-endeavour to realise and grasp the hidden meaning of existence. Faith, in India, did not mean a cosy belief to rest by, but a torch to set the soul on fire with a longing for spiritual realisation. In the absence of this longing and struggle, the belief of the faithful does not differ from the unbelief of the faithless. Belief with most people is simply another name for mental laziness. Religious earnestness with people of this class means, especially when organised under a militant church or a theocratic state, either the pursuit of aggressive religious proselytism or of *jehads* and crusades. They cannot understand the meaning of that earnestness which proceeds from an inner spiritual hunger. No dogma or creed or frenzied acts can satisfy this hunger of a religious heart. Its only bread is spiritual realisation. Religion is a matter of inner experience, a coming in touch with spiritual facts, and not a matter of belief or dogma or conformity.

Strengthened by the spirit of the Upaniṣads, no all-powerful church, therefore, rose in India to organise the faithful on the basis of dogma and creed, and claiming divine authority for its opinions and judgements. No such authority could thrive where religion was expounded as a quest and not a conformity. A spiritual view of religion, as different from a creedal or dogmatic view, makes religion not only cultivate a spirit of toleration, questioning, and inquiry in its own sphere, but also foster it in every other department of life. The *Bhagavad-Gītā* (VI. 44) declares that a spirit of inquiry into the meaning of religion takes an aspirant beyond the authority of the words of scripture and mandate of tradition. He becomes an experimenter himself, instead of remaining a mere believer. Indian religious thought emphasises *sādhanā,* experiment, as the dynamics of religion; it has recourse to *jijñāsā,* or inquiry, for the formulation of its views, be it *Brahma-jijñāsā,* inquiry into the nature of Brahman, i.e. God as the one Self of all, or *dharma-jijñāsā,* inquiry into *dharma,* i.e., social ethics and personal morality.

This sublime attitude to religion and thought is the fruit of the unified view of the mental life of man which India learned from her Upaniṣads, and which she assimilated into her mind and mood by a universal acceptance of all forms of faith and by showing due regard to all knowledge, whether sacred or secular.

10. *'Vidyā Dadāti Vinayam—Knowledge Bestows Humility'*

Science in the modern age has lengthened man's intellectual tether, but this has only helped to bring into sharper focus the mystery of the unknown and the significance of the *parā vidyā* (higher knowledge or wisdom) of which the Upaniṣads speak. In the words of J. Arthur Thomson (*Introduction to Science,* Home University Library edition, 1934, p. 205) :

> 'At the end of his intellectual tether, man has never ceased to become religious.'

It is no wonder, therefore, that several scientists during the last few decades, have been forced to overstep the limits of their sciences and tackle the problem of the unknown at closer quarters in a mood of humility and reverence, illustrating the dictum of Indian wisdom : *'Vidyā dadāti vinayam*—knowledge bestows humility', and the saying of Coleridge quoted by J. Arthur Thomson (*ibid.*, p. 208) :

> 'All knowledge begins and ends with wonder ; but the first wonder is the child of ignorance ; the second wonder is the parent of adoration.'

Dogmatism and cock-sureness which stifle the

spirit of free inquiry are as much enemies of true science as of true religion. There are not wanting scientists today who would, taking a narrow view of the scope and function of science, prefer to go the dogmatic way and cry halt to advancing knowledge and unified experience. That way spells danger to science now, as it has spelt danger to religion before. *A greater devotion to the spirit of free inquiry and a broader conception of the aim and temper of science is our only safeguard against such a pitfall.*

If the nineteenth century was the century of conflict and division, the twentieth century bids fair to become the century of reconciliation and union, as a result of a sincere effort on the part of both science and religion to reassess itself and to understand the other. The humility of twentieth-century physical science presents a sharp and welcome contrast to the cock-sureness of its nineteenth century counterpart. It has realised that the spirit of free inquiry, on which it has thrived, may find expression in fields beyond its own narrow departments, and that it is this spirit, unbiased by personal attachments and aversions, that makes a study scientific, and not the mere subject-matter of that study.

This wider view of science as a discipline and a temper enables us to class as scientific, the study of the facts of the inner world which religion has set to itself for inquiry.

And this has been the Indian approach to religion. It was the absence of this approach that made religion in the West less and less equipped to meet the challenge of advancing knowledge.

11. Limitations of Physical Science

When we go deeper into the nature and scope of physical science, its limitations become apparent. To illustrate : Two branches of science, namely, physics, including astronomy, and biology, including behaviouristic psychology, have given us a vast body of knowledge regarding the nature of the universe and man. Up to the end of the nineteenth century, physics was warped in its final judgements. It saw materialism and mechanism reigning supreme in the universe. There was then a cock-sureness in its pronouncements ; but, in the twentieth century, an element of humility is discernible in the attitude of the great physicists of the age. In the nineteenth century, knowledge of the physical world was not deep enough, and scientists looked only at the surface of things. But, along with the discovery of such facts as radio-activity and insight into the nucleus of the atom, the realisation has come that there is a severe limitation placed on our knowledge regarding the truth of the external world. Science owns today that it deals only with *the appearances of things* and not with *the reality behind these appearances.* Some of the greatest of modern physicists tell us that what science has revealed of the world around us is only the outer aspect of things. Behind this *observable* universe, there is an *unobservable* universe, as well as the *observer* himself. This is a great confession of the limitations of science and its methods. Science is dealing with phenomena revealed by the senses or by apparatuses helpful to the senses. But these senses reveal so little, and what they reveal only tells us that there are realities behind the sense world determining it and controlling it. Physical science restricts itself to the understanding of the observable part of the universe and to controlling its energies for the use of man.

A similar situation obtains in the science of biology. In the last century, it was cock-sure about its pronouncements. By a study of the different aspects of the phenomena of life, it arrived at the great theory of evolution, from which it drew certain conclusions influenced by the mechanistic materialism of contemporary physics, which directly led to a form of materialism, that equated man with the animal, and both to a machine. Today, scientists tell us that they were not happy titles that Darwin chose for his famous books : *The Origin of Species* and *The Descent of Man.* Sir Julian Huxley suggests that these could have been more appropriately titled : *The Evolution of Organisms* and *The Ascent of Man* (*Evolution after Darwin,* Vol. I, The University of Chicago Press, p. 17). But, then, these books appeared at a time when a fierce controversy was going on between emerging science and the entrenched Christian dogma of supernaturalism upholding man as a special creation of an extra-cosmic God, and this had its impact even on the choosing of the titles of great scientific books. The science of physics with its thorough-going materialism and mechanistic determinism, and the science of biology with its newly discovered evolutionary theory and its domination by the general materialistic outlook of science and scientists of the age, helped to shatter nineteenth century man's faith in that view of religion and spiritual values which was presented to the West as supernatural and antiscience.

The limitations of physical science, admitted by many modern scientists themselves, proceed from the adjective *physical,* but science itself is not limited similarly. Reality may be studied, but not exhausted, by the physical sciences, whose limitations proceed from their dependence entirely on sense-data. This limitation has been pointed out by the mathematician-astronomer, the late Sir Arthur Eddington (*The Philosophy of Physical Science*, p. 16):

'Let us suppose that an ichthyologist is exploring the life of the ocean. He casts a net into the water and brings up a fishy assortment. Surveying his catch, he proceeds, in the usual manner of a scientist, to systematise what it reveals. He arrives at two generalisations:

1. No sea-creature is less than two inches long:
2. All sea-creatures have gills.

These are both true of his catch, and he assumes tentatively that they will remain true however often he repeats it. . . . His generalisation is perfectly true of the class of creatures he is talking about—a selected class perhaps, but he would not be interested in making generalisations about any other class.'

Earlier, Eddington, had said in his Preface to the above book (*ibid.* p. ix):

'I am not among those who think that, in the search for truth, all aspects of human experience are to be ignored, save those which are followed up in physical science. But I find no disharmony between a philosophy which embraces the wider significance of human experience and the specialised philosophy of physical science, even though the latter relates to a system of thought of recent growth whose stability is yet to be tested.'

12. *'Materialism an Intruder'*

When physical science or scientists forget or ignore this limitation implied in the adjective 'physical', and pronounce judgements on life or reality as a whole, it or they become dogmatic, and forsake truth-seeking ; one such dogma that is stifling the spirit of modern physical science is *materialism,* against which distinguished scientists have protested and warned. After terming materialism *an intruder* earlier in his book *Methods and Results* (Volume I, p. 161), Thomas Huxley, the collaborator of Darwin, repudiates materialism as a philosophy of life (*ibid.*, pp. 164-65) :

'If we find that the ascertainment of the order of nature is facilitated by using one terminology or one set of symbols, rather than another, it is our clear duty to use the former ; and no harm can accrue, so long as we bear in mind that we are dealing merely with terms and symbols. . . .

'But the man of science who, forgetting the limits of philosophical inquiry, slides from these formulae and symbols into what is commonly understood by materialism, seems to me to place himself on a level with the mathematician who should mistake the *x*'s and *y*'s with which he works the problems for real entities—and with this further disadvantage, as compared with the mathematician, that the blunders of the latter are of no practical consequence, *while the errors of systematic materialism may paralyse the energies and destroy the beauty of a life.'* (italics not by the author).

13. Physical Science and the Mystery of the Universe

The universe was a mystery to man in the primitive stage ; it has not ceased to be so for civilised man even in this twentieth century. We find scientists like the late Sir James Jeans writing books on the scientific view of the universe with such titles as *The Mysterious Universe*. If, after all these marvellous scientific discoveries and inventions, the scientist still treats nature as profoundly mysterious, if, in spite of all the vast knowledge that he has gained, the scientist feels that he has only scratched the surface of nature, that he is yet far far away from the heart of the problem of the universe, we have to pause and ask the question as framed by Śaṅkarācārya : *tataḥ kiṁ tataḥ kim*—'What else ? What next ?' Says Sir James Jeans in his *The New Background of Science* (p. 68) :

'Physical science set out to study a world of matter and radiation, and finds that it cannot describe or picture the nature of either, even to itself. Photons, electrons, and protons have become about as meaningless to the physicist as *x, y, z* are to a child on its first day of learning algebra. The most we hope for at the moment is to discover ways of manipulating *x, y, z* without knowing what they are, with the result that the advance of knowledge is at present reduced to what Einstein has described as extracting one incomprehensible from another incomprehensible.'

14. Physical Science and the Mystery of Man

Even while confronted by, and engaged in tackling, the mystery of the external universe, modern science has become impressed with a deeper mystery, the mystery of man himself, the challenge of the inner world of man. His physical dimension poses no challenge to a science which has achieved revolutionary advances in its branches of anatomy and physiology, neurology and microbiology, medicine and behaviouristic psychology. But these point out to a mysterious depth in him which reveals a new dimension to nature herself, namely, her *within,* over and above her *without.*

Man reveals dimensions that cannot be reduced to the merely physical, the merely material. These latter are his 'not-self' aspects which enter into the constitution of his body, which obviously is just a speck of dust in that vast world of the not-self, but there is in him also something transcendental, which cannot be so reduced. He is the self ; that is his primary inalienable aspect. And if science is to progress further, it has to choose for investigation this field of the mystery of man which towers over its erstwhile study, namely, the mystery of the external universe. This is a vast field of study—the field of man's self-awareness, the field of his consciousness, his ego, his being the *subject* and not the object. Science will find here a vaster and more fascinating and rewarding field of study than in external nature. Already scientists in the West are slowly turning their attention to this great mystery, that of *Man the Unknown,* in the words of the American scientist the late Alexis Carrel, apart from that of *Man the Known,* which is the subject of the positive sciences like physics, chemistry, biology and behaviouristic psychology.

15. Physics and the Mystery of Man

Man is the creator of science and technology, culture and civilisation ; he is also today the only possible destroyer of his civilisation. Everything about him is a mystery. As Lincoln Barnett says in his study of Einstein's contribution to modern scientific thought (*The Universe and Dr. Einstein*, Mentor edition, pp. 126-27) :

'In the evolution of scientific thought, one fact has become impressively clear; there is no mystery of the physical world which does not point to a mystery beyond itself. All highroads of the intellect, all byways of theory and conjecture, lead ultimately to an abyss that human ingenuity can never span. For man is enchained by the very condition of his being, his finiteness and involvement in nature. The further he extends his horizons, the more vividly he recognises the fact that, as the physicist Niels Bohr puts it, "We are both spectators and actors in the great drama of existence". *Man is thus his own greatest mystery.* He does not understand the vast veiled universe into which he has been cast for the reason that he does not understand himself. He comprehends but little of his organic processes and even less of his unique capacity to perceive the world around him, to reason and to dream. *Least of all does he understand his noblest and most mysterious faculty : the ability to transcend himself and perceive himself in the act of perception.*' (italics not by the author).

Or, as expressed by the mathematician-mystic Pascal :

'In space, the universe engulfs me and reduces me to a pin-point. But through thought, I understand that universe.'

16. *Biology and the Mystery of Man*

Pleading for the viewing of man in his depths on the part of modern science, the eminent paleontologist, the late Pere Teilhard de Chardin says (*The Phenomenon of Man,* Collins, London, 1959, pp. 35-36) :

'When studied narrowly in himself by anthropologists or jurists, man is a tiny, even a shrinking, creature. His over-pronounced individuality conceals from our eyes the whole to which he belongs ; as we look at him, our minds incline to break nature up into pieces and to forget both its deep inter-relations and its measureless horizons. We incline to all that is bad in anthropocentrism. And it is this that leads scientists to refuse to consider man as an object of scientific scrutiny except through his body.

'The time has come to realise that an interpretation of the universe—even a positivist one—remains unsatisfying unless it covers the interior as well as the exterior of things ; mind as well as matter. *The true physics is that which will, one day, achieve the inclusion of man in his wholeness in a coherent picture of the world.*' (italics not by the author).

The Upaniṣads of India discovered the finite man as but the outer crust or layer of the infinite and immortal man within. In his finiteness, he enters, and is entered into by, the finite world of myriad changes around him. In this, he is a *speck of dust* in the vast immensity of space in which 'the universe engulfs me and reduces me to a pin-point', in the profound words of Pascal quoted above. But in his infinite dimension as the imperishable Self, he *understands* the universe and also *transcends* it. The dimensions of this inner aspect of man and, through him, of his environing universe, are slowly dawing on modern scientific thought.

Asking the significant question : 'Up to now has science ever troubled to look at the world other than from without ?' (*ibid.*, p. 52), Chardin proceeds to say (*ibid.*, p. 55) :

> 'In the eyes of the physicist, nothing exists legitimately, at least up to now, except the without of things. The same intellectual attitude is still permissible in the bacteriologist, whose cultures (apart from substantial difficulties) are treated as laboratory reagents. But it is still more difficult in the realm of plants. It tends to become a gamble in the case of a biologist studying the behaviour of insects or coelenterates. It seems merely futile with regard to the vertebrates. Finally, it breaks down completely with man, in whom the existence of a within can no longer be evaded, because it is the object of a direct intuition and the substance of all knowledge.'

The world outside, as much as most people in India itself, do not yet know that it was the higher part of, what Julian Huxley terms, *a science of human possibilities,* that India developed ages ago in her Upaniṣads and the *Gītā,* and has continued to foster, up to our own times, as Vedānta and Yoga, as the *adhyātma-vidyā,* the *vidyā,* or science, of man in depth, the science and technique of a comprehensive spirituality encompassing action as well as contemplation. *Indian philosophy sees no conflict between physical sciences and this science of spirituality, between 'man, the known' and 'man, the unknown', between the physical man and the spiritual man.*

And Chardin concludes (*ibid.*, p. 56) :

> 'It is impossible to deny that, deep within ourselves, an "Interior" appears at the heart of beings, as it were seen through a rent. This is enough to ensure that, in one degree or another, this "interior" should obtrude itself as existing everywhere in nature from all time. Since the stuff of the universe has an inner aspect at one point of itself, there is necessarily a double aspect to its structure, that is to say, in every region of space and time—in the same way, for instance, as it is granular : coextensive with their *without*, there is a *within* to things.'

It is high time that our people today, particularly our teachers and students, turn their critical attention, interest, and inquiry, and direct their searchlight of research, into this fascinating and rewarding constituent of their hoary national tradition, into the mystery of this inner dimension of nature revealed in nature's unique product, namely, man. If man does not acquire this strength of spirituality from within, he will have to depend more and more on external sources for stabilising himself. Such external dependence, for clinical purposes occasionally, is understandable. But to make it the normal pattern of human life *is to drain human life of all spiritual values and to surrender human destiny to social engineering techniques such as of molecular biology, and convert human society to an animal farm.* That such dismal possibilities are there before man, due to a wholesale dependence on physical sciences and technology, is revealed in recent books with grim titles like *The Biological Time Bomb* by G. Ratray Taylor. *The science that will do so will cease to be science and become ne-science!*

As we advance into this inquiry and research into our tradition, we shall get an increasing grip on the human situation in our country, through the reformulation and implementation of educational goals and processes in the light of our own philosophy of man, whereby a happy synthesis of physical sciences with the science of spirituality will be achieved, resulting in total human enrichment, internal as well as external, qualitative as well as quantitative.

Says the great neurologist, Sir Charles Sherrington (*Man on His Nature,* Pelican edition, p. 38) :

'Today, Nature looms larger than ever and includes more fully than ever ourselves. It is, if you will, a machine, but it is a partly mentalised machine and in virtue of including ourselves, it is a machine with human qualities of mind. It is a running stream of energy —mental and physical—and unlike man-made machines, it is actuated by emotions, fears, and hopes, dislikes and love.'

17. Evolution: Organic versus Psycho-social

In a lecture on 'The Evolutionary Vision', delivered in 1959 at the closing session of the Chicago University symposium on 'Evolution after Darwin', held to commemorate the centenary of the publication of Darwin's *Origin of Species,* the noted biologist, the late Sir Julian Huxley, gave a spiritual orientation to the evolutionary process (*Evolution after Darwin,* Vol. III, pp. 251-52) :

'Man's evolution is not biological but psycho-social; it operates by the mechanism of cultural tradition, which involves the cumulative self-reproduction and self-variation of mental activities and their products. Accordingly, major steps in the human phase of evolution are achieved by breakthroughs to new dominant patterns of mental organisation of knowledge, ideas and beliefs—ideological instead of physiological or biological organisation. ...

'All dominant thought organisations are concerned with the ultimate, as well as with the immediate, problems of existence or, I should rather say, with the most ultimate problems that the thought of the time is capable of formulating or even envisaging. They are all concerned with giving some interpretation of man, of the world which he is to live in, and of his place and role in that world—in other words, some comprehensive picture of human destiny and significance.'

Further, Huxley reveals the trend of evolution, at the human stage, towards *quality* (*ibid.*, Vol. III, pp. 261-62) :

'It (evolutionary vision) shows us mind enthroned above matter, quantity subordinate to quality.'

In his essay on 'Emergence of Darwinism', Huxley sums up the goal of the evolutionary process at the human level as *fulfilment* (*ibid.*, Vol. I, p. 20) :

'In the light of our present knowledge, man's most comprehensive aim is seen not as mere survival, not as numerical increase, not as increased complexity of organisation or increased control over his environment, but as greater fulfilment—the fuller realisation of more possibilities by the human species collectively and more of its component members individually.'

And pleading for the development of a *science of human possibilities,* Huxley further says (*ibid.*, Vol. I, p. 21) :

'Once greater fulfilment is recognised as man's ultimate or dominant aim, we shall need a science of human possibilities to help guide the long course of psycho-social evolution that lies ahead.'

18. *Psycho-social Evolution*

What is meant by psycho-social evolution? From the living cell up to man, biological evolution was motivated by organic satisfactions, numerical increase, and organic survival. But with the appearance of man, these become, says modern biology, secondary and not primary ; the primary motivation becomes *fulfilment* : and evolution itself becomes, at the stage of man, conscious and deliberate and goal-oriented, unlike the blind processes at the pre-human stages. This revolutionary change is the result of the fully developed cerebral system in man, in virtue of which the evolutionary process itself undergoes a revolutionary change ; *what was organic evolution becomes psycho-social evolution.* Organic evolution has no primary significance in the case of man endowed by nature with the versatile cerebral organ, with the aid of which he can invent any organs he may need more efficiently and quickly than what nature can do for him through her slow and wasteful evolutionary processes. Accordingly, evolution has risen from its organic to the psycho-social level in man, says biology.

In a self-centred man, as in all pre-human species, the psyche or mind or soul is limited and confined to the physical organism. In a moral or ethical man, it expands, goes beyond the limitations of his physical organism and enters, and is entered into by, other psyches of the social *milieu.* This is the fruit of psycho-social evolution. What biology calls psycho-social evolution is what the science of religion calls ethical awareness and social feeling, the by-product of the early phases of the *spiritual growth* of man.

With the onset of this psycho-social evolution, men develop the capacity to dig affections into each other *as a matter of conscious choice,* thus revealing a higher dimension to the human individuality than what is revealed by his physical individuality with its organic appetities and choices. All ethical theories presuppose a distinction between a lower self and a higher self in man ; and the liberation of the higher self is what man achieves through psycho-social evolution or spiritual growth ; it is renunciation of the lower self and manifestation of the higher self.

The subject of the spiritual growth of man, of evolution as psycho-social, is a pregnant theme to man in the modern age. It points out to him the way to rescue himself from the tyranny of the sensate and the quantitative, and from the prevailing stagnation of worldliness, and helps him to continue his evolutionary march to *qualitative* richness and fulfilment, individually and collectively.

The initial focus of self in man is the ego, which appears on the evolutionary scene only with the appearance of man ; and even at the stage of man, it appears only after the human infant is about two or two-and-a-half years old. And it is significant to note that, till its appearance, the human infant is as helpless and dependent on the environment like all pre-human species and that, with its appearance, the infant begins to dominate the environment. A human child of four or five years of age can control and manage animals like horses or other cattle immensely larger physically than itself. Modern neurology attributes this unique phenomenon to the emergence of a new datum in the human child, with new capacities and energies as its fruit; that datum is the self as the ego and those capacities are imagination, reason, judgement, will, etc. Referring to this, neurologist Grey Walter says (*The Living Brain*, p. 2):

'Thus the mechanisms of the brain reveal a deep physiological division between man and ape. ... If the title of soul be given to the higher functions in question, it must be admitted that the other animals have only a glimmer of the light that so shines before men. ...The nearest creature to us, the chimpanzee, cannot retain an image long enough to reflect on it, however clever it may be in learning tricks or getting food that is placed beyond its natural reach. Unable to rehearse the possible consequences of different responses to a stimulus, without any faculty of planning, the apes and other animals cannot learn to control their feelings, the first step towards independence of environment and eventual control of it. The activity of the animal brain is not checked to allow time for the choice of one among several possible responses, but only for the one reflex or conditioned response to emerge. The monkey's brain is in thrall to its senses. *Sentio ergo sum* (I sense, therefore I exist) might be the first reflection of a slightly inebriated ape, as it is often the last of alcoholic man; so near and yet so far apart, even then, are they.

'The brain of lion, tiger, rhinoceros, and other powerful animals also lack the mechanism of imagination, or we should not be here to discuss the matter. They cannot envisage changes in their environment, so they have never sought to alter it in all their efforts to retain lordship of their habitat.'

Man alone achieved this power of *imaging* ideas ; and this power was not an isolated phenomenon in him. Within the increased area of the cortex of the ancestral organ, nature evolved for man capacities for a series of new processes : observation, memory, comparison, evaluation, selection, judgement, and deliberate action. And in achieving these, he achieved two things :

Firstly, *discovery of the path leading to the processing of raw experience into knowledge, of knowledge into power, and power into control and manipulation of the environment constituted of the not-self aspect of experience.*

Secondly, *a faint awareness of the reality of himself as the subject, as the self, behind the fleeting images in his mind, and the discovery of the road leading inward to the total comprehension of this new dimension of reality, resulting in the increasing liberation of moral, aesthetic, and spiritual values in his life, action, and behaviour.*

Man's steady advance on these two fronts constitutes the story of culture and civilisation ; it constitutes also the march of evolution at the post-human stage. With the emergence, on the evolutionary scene, of the mind of man against the background of self-awareness, and disciplined in the seeking and finding of knowledge of the self and the not-self in varying degrees, nature yields, in increasing measure, to one of her own products, the control and manipulation of the evolutionary process.

19. Rising from Knowledge to Wisdom

In spite of his rudimentary self-knowledge which gave him a measure of control of the animal and natural world, the earliest man largely remained an animal in appetites and behaviour. A little more of this self-knowledge, gained through reflection in the context of social experience, helped to increase his control over himself and to humanise him. This process, ever in operation in human cultures and civilisations and socio-political organisations, has led up to the man of the modern age, with his almost total control over the not-self environment through an efficient technology, with his global sweep in socio-cultural interests and contacts, and with his yearning for the universal and human.

Yet, the disparity between his knowledge of his self and control over his inner nature, on the one hand, and his knowledge of and control over the external nature, on the other, between, in short, his moral efficiency and his technical efficiency, confronts him with the most serious problem that his evolution has so far seriously posed. This is thwarting his urges and efforts to achieve fulfilment. Neglected and unsolved, this problem may as well make him the only possible destroyer of his civilisation, of the fruits of evolution, and of his species as well. In the meantime, he is destined to move from one tension to another, from one sorrow and unfulfilment to another.

The only solution lies in the deepening and strengthening of his moral and spiritual awareness. Biological evolution achieved a measure of this in the life of earliest man in his rudimentary knowledge of his own self. Social evolution, guided by human intelligence, advanced this still further, by which a physical and organic self, separated from all other selves, gave place to a social self, morally related to an increasing number of other human beings. *The dynamism of human evolution demands that this education of man must contnnue till he rises from ego-centredness to ego-transcendence, and from knowledge to wisdom.* Referring to this urgent need to rise from knowledge to wisdom, the late Bertrand Russell says (*The Impact of Science on Society,* pp. 120-21) :

'We are in the middle of a race between human skill as to means and human folly as to ends. Given sufficient folly as to ends, every increase in the skill required to achieve them is to the bad. The human race has survived hitherto owing to ignorance and incompetence; but, given knowledge and competence combined with folly, there can be no certainty of survival. Knowledge is power, but it is power for evil just as much as for good. It follows that, *unless men increase in wisdom as in knowledge, increase of knowledge will be increase of sorrow.*' (italics not by the author).

Biology speaks of the principle of homeostasis, or homeorhesis, as clarified by biologist Waddington, by which nature effected an automatic stabilisation of internal conditions in the organism of the higher mammals. This helped in the slow evolution of the brain until, in man, she perfected the higher brain. The organism's need for physical survival and organic satisfactions, and her own need for numerical increase—all these have been relegated by nature to the care of man's lower brain, thus releasing his higher brain, 'for functions surpassing the wonders of homeostasis itself', according to modern neurology (*The Living Brain,* p. 16), or to function as the most wonderful instrument for carrying evolution to its specifically human fields, namely, the psycho-social, or the moral and the spiritual, according to Vedānta.

20. *Psycho-social Evolution as Spiritual Growth*

The capacity and fitness of the higher brain to undertake and fulfil this high function is directly proportional to its freedom from thraldom to his lower brain, from slavery to his sensory apparatus and its appetites, from the pressures and pulls of his lower nature. It is obvious that his higher brain, with its powers of imagination and reason, may stultify itself by functioning as the *tail-end* of the sensory apparatus and of the lower brain. It may, on the other hand, redeem itself, and also become true to itself, by becoming truly higher. It is ethical discipline, what Vedānta calls *śama* and *dama*, discipline of the mind and discipline of the senses, that helps the higher brain to thus redeem itself, and become the agent also of man's redemption. *This is human reason and will in its true form,* what Vedānta calls *buddhi,* the supreme instrument which lifts life from knowledge to wisdom and from bondage to freedom. Referring to the significance, through homeostasis, of this development of the higher brain, Grey Walter claims (*ibid.*, p. 18) :

'For mammals all, homeostasis meant survival ; but for man, emancipation.'

Thus the spiritual growth of man is a fact. And the more we know the science and technique of this growth, the better for us and for our society. Growth, both the concept and the word, is of protean significance. We know and recognise two types of human growth, namely, physical and mental, the second less palpably than the first. A baby at birth is about seven pounds in body weight ; and every day it increases in weight. It drinks its mother's milk, to be followed by other types of food and drink ; and it grows steadily until it becomes a full-frown healthy man or woman of 70 or 80 kilos weight. This is the palpable physical growth of man ; and we ensure it by appropriate physical nourishment accompanied with exercise. Equally important, though less obvious, is his mental growth. Through education, a human child grows in alertness, self-confidence, and a sense of individual worth and dignity ; this growth continues till he becomes an intellectual giant or a giant of will. This is the mental growth of man which we ensure through appropriate mental nourishment—through education, institutional and non-institutional.

These two types of growth are necessary, but not sufficient. There is a third type of growth, most vital and significant, but least recognised, without which the other two will prove his undoing, individually and collectively, without which his craving and search for fulfilment will only result in unfulfilment and defeat. This is his spiritual growth, or growth in his spiritual dimension, which finds expression in ethical awareness and social feeling to begin with, and finds, according to Vedānta, its consummation in the experience, by him, of the infinite, universal, and divine dimension of his individuality, the Ātman.

21. Status of the Ego in Evolution

The ego that made man dominate nature is not his true self, but only an initial datum, a promise of greater things to come. It is like the tip of a rock seen above the water level, with the immense rock mass itself lying unseen, and waiting to be revealed, below the water level. The real Self of man, says India's *adhyātma-vidyā,* science of man as the Ātman, is inaccessible to the sense organs and to the sense-bound mind, but accessible to the *buddhi,* or reason, when it becomes subtle and pure—*buddhi-grāhyam, atīndriyam,* as the *Gītā* expresses it. That the ego is unreal, that man's individuality or selfhood does not consist in the ego, is the central truth also of Buddhism ; and this is affirmed by modern biology also. In the words of *The Science of Life,* a voluminous digest of modern biological knowledge by H. G. Wells, G. P. Wells, and Julian Huxley, in its section dealing with the philosophical implications of biology (pp. 878-79) :

'Alone, in the silence of the night, and on a score of thoughtful occasions, we have demanded : can this self, so vividly central to my universe, so greedily possessive of the world, ever cease to be ? Without it, surely, there is no world at all ! And yet, this conscious self dies nightly when we sleep, and we cannot trace the stages by which in its stages it crept to an awareness of its own existence.

'Personality (centred in the ego) may be only one of nature's methods, a convenient provisional delusion of considerable strategic value. . . .

'The more intelligent and comprehensive man's picture of the universe has become, the more intolerable has become his concentration on the individual life with its inevitable final rejection. . . .

'He escapes from his ego by this merger (identification with and participation in a greater being), and acquires an impersonal immortality in the association, his identity dissolving into the greater identity. This is the essence of much religious mysticism, and it is remarkable how closely the biological analysis of individuality brings us to the mystics. . . .

'The Western mystic and the Eastern sage find a strong effect of endorsement in modern science and the everyday teaching of practical morality ; both teach that self must be subordinated, that self is a method and not an end.'

The science and technique of spiritual growth, from the 'convenient provisional delusion' of the ego to the true self, is the special contribution of ethics, aesthetics, and religion. It provides spiritual nourishment to man both when he is at work and when he is at worship, when he is in society and when he is alone. Work done in a spirit of service and dedication, reinforced by an inward penetration through worship and meditation, through *bhakti* and *bhajan,* forms the twin technique of spiritual growth, according to Śrī Kṛṣṇa's teaching in the *Gītā* (VIII. 7) :

> *Tasmāt sarveṣu kāleṣu*
> *māmanusmara, yuddhya ca—*

'Therefore, at all times, meditate upon Me, and engage yourself in the battle (of life)' ; and, again, in verse 55 of chapter XI, introducing which Śaṅkarācārya says :

> *Adhunā sarvasya gītā-śāstrasya*
> *sāra-bhūto artho niḥśreyasārtho*
> *anuṣṭheyatvena samuccitya ucyate—*

'Now is proclaimed the practical implications of the essence of the meaning of the entire science of the *Gītā* designed to lead one to spiritual freedom' :

Matkarmakṛt, mat-paramo,
mat bhaktaḥ saṅga-varjitaḥ ;
Nirvairaḥ sarvabhūteṣu
yaḥ sa māmeti Pāṇḍava—

'Perform work (in a spirit of dedication) to Me ; make Me the supreme goal (of your life) ; be My devotee, free from attachment and enmity to all beings ; such (a seeker) attains to Me alone, O Arjuna.'

The laboratory for this science of spiritual growth is life itself, with its twin arenas of work outside and meditation within. The temple or church or mosque outside, or the worship room within the house, properly used, also provides another laboratory. More important than these two is the laboratory of a trained and pure mind. Worship and rituals and other religious practices form useful aids, if they are not done as items of a static piety, not done as ends in themselves, but as means to spiritual growth, as instruments of a dynamic spirituality, as a depth education for character.

22. *Kinship between Ancient Vedānta and Modern Science*

Swami Vivekananda has shown that religion, as developed in India in her Vedānta, and modern science, are close to each other in spirit and temper and objectives. Both are spiritual disciplines. Even in the cosmology of the physical universe, in the theory of the unity of cause and effect, in the unity and conservation of matter and energy, and in the concept of evolution, cosmic and organic, the two reveal many points of contract. Unlike as in the *super*-naturalistic theologies of the West, the fundamental position in the cosmology of both Vedānta and modern science is, what Swami Vivekananda calls, 'the postulate (of the ultimate reality), of a self-evolving cause'. Vedānta calls it Brahman, which is a universal spiritual principle. The *Taittirīya Upaniṣad* (III. 1) defines Brahman in a majestic utterance, which will be welcomed by every scientific thinker :

Yato vā imāni bhūtāni jāyante,
yena jātāni jīvanti ;
yat prayantyabhisaṁviśanti ;
tadvijijñāsasva ; tad brahmeti—

'Wherefrom all these entities are born, by which, being born, they abide ; into which, at the time of dissolution, they enter—seek to know That ; That is Brahman.'

To the modern scientist, that self-evolving cause is a material reality, the *background material* or *cosmic dust,* as astrophysicist Fred Hoyle terms it ; whereas, to Vedānta, *which views it also in the light of the consciousness revealed in its evolutionary product, namely, man,* it is a universal spiritual principle, the *cit ākāśa.*

Referring to this spiritual kinship between modern science and ancient Vedānta, Swami Vivekananda said in his speech at the Parliament of Religions held at Chicago in 1893 (*Complete Works,* Vol. I, eleventh edition, p. 15) :

> 'Manifestation, and not creation, is the word of science today, and the Hindu is only glad that what he has been cherishing in his bosom for ages is going to be taught in more forcible language, and with further light, from the latest conclusions of science.'

Although modern scientific thought does not yet have, like Vedānta, a recognised place for any spiritual reality or principle, several scientists of the twentieth century, including biologists like Teilhard de Chardin and Julian Huxley, as pointed out earlier, have endeavoured to soften the materialism of physical science and to find a place for spiritual experience in the scientific world picture. Even Thomas Huxley, as quoted earlier, had termed materialism *an intruder.* In this century, this protest has come from great physicists also. Sir James Jeans found that the final picture of the universe emerging from twentieth-century physical science was one in which the notion of matter was completely eliminated, 'mind reigning supreme and alone' (*The New Background of Science*, p. 307). Astrophysicist R. A. Millikan considered materialism 'a philosophy of unintelligence' (*An Autobiography*, last chapter).

23. Philosophy : Synthesis of Science and Religion

If twentieth-century physics is thus turning its face away from thoroughgoing materialism, twentieth-century biology is not behind it in this orientation. The whole of modern scientific thought is in the throes of a silent spiritual revolution with the emergence, on the horizon of scientific thought, of the challenge of mind and consciousness, and the consequent need to deveolp, what Jeans terms, *a new background of science* in the light of what he says further (*The New Background of Science*, pp. 2-6) :

'The old philosophy ceased to work at the end of the nineteenth century, and the twentieth-century physicist is hammering out a new philosophy for himself. Its essence is that he no longer sees nature as something entirely distinct from himself. Sometimes it is what he himself creates or selects or abstracts; sometimes it is what he destroys.

'Thus the history of physical science in the twentieth-century is one of a progressive emancipation from the purely human angle of vision.'

Julian Huxley and Chardin find the spiritual character of the world-stuff successively revealed in the course of organic evolution. Biology, in its theory of evolution, they hold, reveals what Chardin calls a *within* to nature, over and above and different from the *without* of nature revealed by physics and astronomy. Vedānta terms the 'within' as the *pratyak rūpa* and the 'without' as the *parāk rūpa* of one and the same nature.

When the significance of this *within* of things is recognised in modern science, the scientific 'background material' will undergo a spiritual orientation and thus come closer to Brahman, the 'background reality' of Vedānta. *The synthesis of the knowledge of the within and the without is philosophy;* and this was what India achieved in her Vedānta ages ago as *saṁyak-jñāna,* comprehensive or perfect knowledge of total Reality. Reality itself does not know any distinction between a within and a without. These distinctions are made only by the human mind for the convenience of study and research and daily life.

As the different branches of the physical sciences are but different approaches to the study of one and the same reality, namely, physical nature, and as all such branches of study, when pursued far enough, tend to mingle and merge into a grand science of the physical universe, *into a unified science of the 'without' of nature,* so the science of the 'within' and the science of the 'without' mingle and merge in a science of Brahman, the total Reality. This is how Vedānta viewed its *Brahmavidyā,* science of Brahman, the term Brahman standing for the totality of Reality, physical and non-physical. The *Muṇḍaka Upaniṣad* (I. i. 1) defines *Brahmavidyā* as *sarva-vidyā pratiṣṭhā,* the *pratiṣṭhā,* or basis, of every *vidyā,* or science. Says Śrī Kṛṣṇa in the *Gītā* (XIII. 2) :

Kṣetra-kṣetrajñayor jñānaṁ
yat tat jñānaṁ mataṁ mama—

'The knowledge of *kṣetra,* the not-self (the 'without' of things), and of *kṣetrajña* the knower of the *kṣetra* (the 'within' of things), is true knowledge, according to Me.'

Dealing with the all-inclusiveness of this Vedāntic thought as expounded by Swami Vivekananda, Romain Rolland says (*The Life of Vivekananda,* p. 289) :

'But it is a matter of indifference to the calm pride of him who deems himself the stronger whether science accepts free Religion, in Vivekananda's sense of the term, or not; for his Religion accepts Science. It is vast enough to find a place at its table for all loyal seekers after truth.'

In his lecture on 'The Absolute and Manifestation' delivered in London in 1896, Swami Vivekananda said (*Complete Works,* Vol. II, ninth edition, p. 140) :

'Do you not see whither science is tending? The Hindu nation proceeded through the study of the mind, through metaphysics and logic. The European nations start from external nature, and now they, too, are coming to the same results. We find that, searching through the mind, we at last come to that Oneness, that universal One, the internal Soul of everything, the essence and reality of everything. ... Through material science, we come to the same Oneness.'

24. Śrī Kṛṣṇa's Synthesis of Science and Religion

The *Śrīmad Bhāgavatam* refers to this complementary character of physical science and the science of religion, with respect to human knowledge and fulfilment, in a profound utterance of Śrī Kṛṣṇa (XI. vii. 19-21) :

Prāyeṇa manujā loke
loka-tattva-vicakṣaṇāḥ ;
Samuddharanti hyātmānam
ātmanaivā- śubhāśayāt—

'Generally, in the world, men who are efficient in the investigation of the truth of the external world or nature, uplift themselves by themselves from all sources of evil.

Âtmano gururātmaiva
puruṣasya viśeṣataḥ ;
Yat pratyakṣānumānābhyāṁ
śreyo'sau anuvindate—

'For a human being, particularly, his *guru* (teacher) is his own self ; because he achieves his welfare through (inquiring into) direct sense experience and (inductive-deductive) inference based on the same.'

Puruṣatve ca māṁ dhīrāḥ
sāṁkhya-yoga-viśāradāḥ ;
Âvistarāṁ prapaśyanti
sarva-śakty-upabṛṁhitam—

'In this very human personality also, wise men, who have mastered the science and art of spirituality, clearly realise Me (God, as the one universal Self of all) as the infinite reservoir of all energies.'

25. *Vedāntic Vision of Evolution*

Vedānta views the entire evolutionary process *as progressive evolution of structure and form, and as greater and greater manifestation of the infinite Self within.* It is evolution of matter and manifestation of spirit. Twentieth-century biology recognises, in the first appearance of living organisms, the emergence, in a rudimentary form, of the unique datum of *experience,* through the unique datum of awareness. The living cell, described by biology as *self-duplicating matter,* discloses the emergence of *experience* as a new value which the immense cosmos never revealed in its billions of years of history.

This spiritual value of awareness 'grows' as it were, in richness and variety, as we move up the evolutionary ladder, defining and enlarging progressively the datum of experience with its two poles of the experiencer and the experienced. The evolution of the nervous system discloses progressive development of awareness in depth and range, and consequent increase in the grip of the organism on its environment.

This awareness achieves a new and significant

breakthrough with the appearance of man on the evolutionary scene. 'Man is unique in more ways than one', says Julian Huxley. The field of awareness of all other organisms is, largely, the external environment and, to a small extent, also the interior of their bodies—the 'without' of nature. Man alone has awareness of the self, as the *subject* of experience, along with awareness of the not-self, as the *object* of experience, of both the *within* and the *without* of nature.

That is the uniqueness of man, according to both twentieth-century biology and ancient Vedānta. Self-awareness, which neurology considers as the source of the dominance of man over all nature, and which nature achieved through the evolution of the human cerebral system, and which remains a minor and hazy pole of experience in the early stages of human evolution, is a new dimension of awareness containing termendous implications, says Indian philosophy, for man's further evolutionary destiny as much as for his philosophy of man and nature.

The Vedāntic view of evolution and of man's uniqueness finds a unique statement in the *Śrīmad Bhāgavatam* (XI. 9. 28) :

Sṛṣṭvā purāṇi vividhā-
nyajayātmaśaktyā

vṛkṣān sarī-sṛpa-paśūn
khaga-daṁśa-matsyān ;
Taistaiḥ atuṣṭa-hṛdayaḥ
puruṣaṁ vidhāya
brahmāvaloka-dhiṣaṇaṁ
mudam āpa devaḥ—

'The divine One, having projected (evolved), with His own inherent power, various forms such as trees, reptiles, cattle, birds, insects and fish, was not satisfied at heart with forms such as these ; He then projected the human form endowed with the capacity to realise Brahman (the universal divine Self of all), and became extremely pleased.'

26. *India's Religious Urge : Realisation and Not Speculation*

Evolution has revealed that the mystery of the universe stirs in man as the mystery of the self. The mystery of the universe will ever remain a mystery until this mystery of the self is cleared. Till then, all our conclusions about the truth of the universe, proceeding from science or philosophy, theology or logic, will be speculative ventures yielding mere postulates and conjectures. The Indian mind was not content to remain at the stage of mere speculation or conjecture in so important a field as the knowledge of the ultimate truth about man and nature. Her thinkers boldly penetrated into the world within, taking the facts of awareness and the ego as the clue, as the *footprints*, in the words of the *Bṛhadāraṇyaka Upaniṣad* (I. 4. 7). And when they penetrated to the depth, they discovered the one infinite and eternal reality behind the finite and the time-bound, and designated that reality as *anubhava svarūpa*, 'of the nature of (infinite) *Experience*', *cit svarūpa*, 'of the nature of *Pure Consciousness*', of which the infinite varieties of objects and subjects in the world are but passing configurations. The *Bṛhadāraṇyaka* registers this approach, and the object of its search, in another significant passage (III. 4. 1) :

Yat sākṣāt aparokṣāt brahma,
ya ātmā sarvāntaraḥ—

'The Brahman that is immediate and direct, the Ātman that is the innermost Self of all.'

'That thou art' (*Tat tvam asi*), proclaims the *Chāndogya Upaniṣad* (VI. viii. 7), aligning mortal man with the immortal divine. Again and again, the Upaniṣads reiterate this great truth. If man as scientist has such a profound dimension that he can comprehend the vast universe in a formula given by his thought, what must be the dimension of man as the Ātman, as Pure Consciousness, as the unchangeable infinite Self ? The Reality that 'remains undivided in the divided things and processes of the world', as the *Gītā* puts it (XIII. 16). The mystery of the universe was finally resolved through the solution of the mystery disclosed within man himself. The sages of the Upaniṣads discovered the centre of the universe in the centre of man. Through that discovery, man was revealed in his infinite dimension ; and the universe was also revealed in all its spiritual glory. Realization of this truth is the only way to life-fulfilment, say the Upaniṣads. Says the *Śvetāśvatara Upaniṣad* (II. 15) :

Yadātma-tattvena tu brahma-tattvam
dīpopameneha yuktaḥ prapaśyet ;
Ajaṁ dhruvaṁ sarvatattvaiḥ viśuddham
jñātvā devaṁ mucyate sarva-pāpaiḥ—

'When the self-controlled spiritual aspirant realises in this very body the truth of Brahman (the infinite Self of all) through the truth of the Ātman (the Self), self-luminous as light, then, knowing the Divinity which is unborn, eternal, and untouched by the modifications of nature, he is freed from all evil.'

This and similar other verses from the Upaniṣads communicate a profound joyous discovery, as can be seen even from the language in which it is couched in that immortal literature. In reaching the ultimate Truth of the Ātman, they had reached also the ultimate of being and knowledge, peace and joy, the unifying *Field of Infinite Experience* itself. Hence they communicated their discovery as the discovery of the inexhaustible mine of *satyam* (truth), *jñānam* (knowledge) and *anantam* (infinitude), or of *sat* (existence), *cit* (knowledge) and *ānanda* (bliss). In the struggle to realise this truth and the life-fulfilment it involves, they saw the true meaning of the entire course of cosmic and organic evolution, especially of human evolution.

The organism seeks fulfilment ; that is the end and aim of all its activities and processes, says modern biology. In the Upaniṣads, we have the beautiful concepts of *mukti,* freedom, and *pūrṇatā,* fullness. We are bound now ; we are fragmented now. We want to become free ; we want to become integral, and experience fullness. Jesus Christ calls it 'perfection' : 'Be ye therefore perfect, even as your Father which is in heaven is perfect' (Matthew, V. 48). To experience the delight of freedom, to enlarge the bounds of man's awareness, to get *bodhi,* complete enlightenment, as the Buddha expressed it, is the great aim of human evolution. Education, science, culture, socio-political processes, and religion are meant to increase and enlarge the bounds of human awareness and the range and depth of human fulfilment, by increasing man's knowledge of, and control over, not only the outside world, but also the deep recesses within himself. Knowledge is power, in the positive sciences ; it is still more so in the science of religion, the science of the inner nature of man, where the power that is gained is not only greater in human terms of quantity, ***but also higher in terms of quality.***

27. *Dharma as Social Ethics*

Man cannot advance on the long road of his spiritual growth, or psycho-social evolution, without *disciplining* his urges for organic satisfactions ; he has to bring a certain measure of stabilisation in his inner life through such discipline, by his own knowledge and efforts ; this is the second homeostasis to be achieved by him, over and above the first homeostasis achieved by nature for him, and to be dealt with in more detail later. It is this second homeostasis that is emphasised by the *Gītā,* namely *samatvaṁ yoga ucyate*—

'*Yoga* is called *samatvam,* equanimity' ; this is the spiritual equivalent of the dictum of the great French physiologist Claude Bernard to be dealt with later : *A fixed interior milieu is the condition for the free life.*

It is this discpline that is indicated in the Indian concept of *dharma,* or ethical sense, which is inseparable from any ordered human society. Bereft of it, man becomes reduced to a beast, says Indian wisdom : *dharmeṇa hīnāḥ paśubhih samānāḥ*. Dharma, as the principle of integration between man and man in society, does not mean religion in the sense of creed, doctrine or ritual, nor any scheme of an other-worldly salvation. A mere accumulation of bricks does not constitute a building ; it needs cement to unite brick to brick to make for its integrated structure. Similarly, a mere aggregation of individuals does not constitute a society ; there is an integrating principle that makes for the evolution of a dynamic and expansive *personality* out of a static *individuality,* and that helps to hold its members together ; and that principle is *dharma* ; it stresses the idea of mutuality, inter-dependence. Man needs the context of other human beings for his very humanisation. This is how Śrī Kṛṣṇa expounds *dharma* in the *Mahābhārata* : *Dhāraṇāt dharma ityāhuḥ, dharmo dhārayate prajāḥ.*

28. *The Puruṣārthas in the Context of Psycho-social Evolution*

Indian spiritual tradition does not frown, or look down, upon *kāma,* organic satisfaction or *artha,* wealth, which is the means to *kāma,* but treats them as valid pursuits, or *puruṣārthas.* But it considers, *lobha,* or greed, and *moha,* or delusion, arising from unchecked organic cravings, as unethical, because they are anti-social. And to restrain these two pursuits from becoming anti-social, it presents a third vital human pursuit, or *puruṣārtha,* namely, *dharma,* ethical sense. It is this third *puruṣārtha,* namely, *dharma,* that helps all people, not just a few powerful and clever ones only, to experience the first two *puruṣārthas,* namely, *kāma* and *artha.* The validity and creative role of *kāma* is presented in the *Gītā* by Śrī Kṛṣṇa, the human manifestation of the one divine Self in all, in his statement (VII. 11) :

Dharmā-viruddho bhūteṣu
kāmo'smi bharatarṣabha—

'I am that *kāma,* sensual desire, in all beings, which is unopposed to *dharma.*'

Indian spiritual tradition refers to *dharma, artha,* and *kāma,* as the *trivarga,* the inseparable group of three, treats them as the universal warp and woof of all ordered human society, theistic, atheistic, or agnostic, and presents *mokṣa,* absolute freedom of the spirit, as the fourth *puruṣārtha,* which is an optional trans-social pursuit meant for those few who desire, and who dare, to go deeper into the spiritual dimensions of reality and realise one's true nature in all its glory. For all the rest, this *mokṣa* experience comes,- within the limitations of the social context, as *dharma. Dharma, thus, is the confluence of the secular and the spiritual, of the social and the trans-social ;* and every sacred and secular literature of India sings its glory. Indian culture is rooted in, and inspired by, this great value of *dharma.* The mystical heights of Indian, and of all world, religions are the expressions of the trans-social *mokṣa* ideal and value.

It is an echo of this great value of *dharma* that we get in the concept of *psycho-social evolution* of twentieth-century biology and in its corollary concepts of *quality* and *fulfilment* as the criteria of evolution at the human stage. And in the emphasis on detachment from the ego, and from the organic system and its cravings centred in it, modern psycho-social evolution echoes the ancient *anāskti-yoga* of the *Gītā.*

29. *Religion : Ethnical versus Spiritual*

A scientific study of religion reveals two dimensions to every religion, especially to every one of the highly developed world religions, namely, religion as a socio-political expression and religion as a path to the experience of God, or any value equivalent to it. The first consists of the do's and don'ts of religion and the rules and regulations about food, dress, marriage, and other social disciplines, besides myths and legends and cosmological theories. These constitute the socio-political constituents of religion, which find a place for it in the census registers and which demarcate it from other religions. It cannot constitute the science of religion but only a historically conditioned socio-political expression of religion. A science of religion will classify religions in terms such as of their *bhakti-yoga, jñāna-yoga, rāja-yoga* and *karma-yoga* contents. This second dimension consists of the truly spiritual part, with its emphasis on personal morality, worship and adoration, and the disciplines designed to ensure the spiritual growth of man. These constitute the essential and the invariable and the universal core of religion, while the former form its variable non-essential part, which is also relevant, but only when it does not choke the spirit of the latter.

Indian tradition calls the former the *smṛti*, and the latter the *śruti,* constituent of a religion, and considers the *śruti* as eternal and universal in validity and the *smṛti* as local, parochial and temporary in application. Accordingly, the *śruti* represents the *sanātana dharma*, eternal religion, which remains, while the *smṛti* represents the *yuga dharma,* the religion for a particular *yuga,* or age, which changes. India, therefore, considers the *yuga dharma* constituent of a religion not only not applicable for all people universally, but even irrelevant to its own people of a later age, due to changes in conditions of life of the people concerned. So Indian tradition provides for appropriate changes in the *smṛtis* and the *yuga dharma,* to make them relevant for the changed social circumstances which render them obsolete, and often harmful. Sri Ramakrishna expresses this Indian wisdom in a brief and meaningful utterance : The Moghul coins have no *currency* under the East India Company's rule. Human and social distortions are the product of the dominance of these obsolete elements of a socio-religious tradition ; they sustain the rigidities of social customs, anti-human practices, inter-religious and intra-religious frictions, disharmonies, and persecutions, and the stagnation and immobility of human attitudes.

The fundamental message of all religions, however, derives from their central core of essential spiritual truths, which constitute their *śruti* element. These spiritual truths are *apauruṣeya,* impersonal, and therefore, universal; they were discovered by the scientists of religion, the mystics. The authenticity of these truths lies in their being experienced by spiritual experimenters *and in their being capable of re-verification by others.* Explaining this authenticity with respect to the Vedas of the Hindu tradition, Swami Vivekananda said in the course of his address at the Chicago Parliament of Religions in 1893 (*Complete Works,* Vol. I, pp. 6-7) :

'By the Vedas no books are meant; they mean the accumulated treasury of spiritual laws discovered by different persons in different times. Just as the law of gravitation existed before its discovery, and would exist if all humanity forgot it, so is it with the laws that govern the spiritual world. The moral, ethical, and spiritual relations between soul and soul, and between individual spirits and the Father of all spirits, were there before their discovery, and would remain even if we forgot them.

'The discoverers of these laws are called ṛṣis (sages), and we honour them as perfected beings. I am glad to tell this audience that some of the very greatest of them were women.'

The above description can be relevant only with respect to the *śruti* constituent of Hinduism, and of every other world religion. The only difference lies in this, that it is only in the Hindu tradition that this distinction between the universality of the *śruti* and the limited relevance of the *smṛti* is fully recognised and applied ; and that social innovators and religious prophets are not only not persecuted and killed, but are honoured and followed. And this blessing Hinduism owes to its immortal literature of the Upaniṣads, which is all *śruti* and with no touch of *smṛti*. They are the only sacred books, both within Hinduism and outside of it, which addressed themselves *exclusively* to the discovery of spiritual truths and to leading man, irrespective of caste, creed, and race, to their realisation in human life, and to the creation in India of a dynamic and healthy climate of active toleration and harmony as the inalienable characteristic of Indian culture and life.

In the light of this *śruti-smṛti* concept, we see the kinship of science only with that aspect of religion as a spiritual path to God, the *śruti* constituent, and very little kinship with its socio-political expression, the *smṛti* constituent. The term *ethnical religion* emphasises the dominance of this *smṛti* element, with its group exclusiveness and tribal loyalties. And it is this ethnical religion that stagnates in course of time, resists social change, and collides against physical science and all creative social endeavour. In all religions, the ethnic element, in course of time, becomes increasingly centred in the priest and the feudal power, and the universal spiritual element is centred in the prophet and the divine incarnation. The ethnical aspect of religion will continue to remain ; but it must be subordinated, says the Hindu tradition, to the spiritual aspect, if it is to aid man in his spiritual growth.

30. India and the Scientific Approach to Religion

The methods of investigation in the field of religion are largely the same as in the positive sciences : Collection of facts, their classification, a dispassionate study of these so as to reveal the law or laws underlying them, such knowledge leading to the control over the phenomena concerned, and, finally, the application of such knowledge for the technique of man's spiritual growth, for the alleviation of human suffering, and for the enrichment and fulfilment of human life. This kind of study of religion, as a thorough scientific study of the facts of the inner life, was undertaken by the great sages of ancient India ; the insights which they gained were re-tested and amplified by a galaxy of subsequent sages, leaving to posterity the invaluable legacy of a rich and dynamic scientific tradition in the field of religion.

It is because of this adamantine, rational, and experiential base that Indian spirituality, and the culture deriving nourishment from it, have stood the test of time. That also explains its hospitality to modern physical science, and its pride in the remarkable achievements of this sister discipline developed by the modern West.

Says Romain Rolland about this quality of Indian philosophical thought (*The Life of Vivekananda*, p. 196) :

> 'The true Vedāntic spirit does not start out with a system of preconceived ideas. It possesses absolute liberty and unrivalled courage among religions with regard to the facts to be observed and the diverse hypotheses it has laid down for their coordination. Never having been hampered by a priestly order, each man has been entirely free to search wherever he pleased for the spiritual explanation of the spectacle of the universe.'

After a thorough investigation into the real nature of man, the sages of the Upanisads made a fundamental discovery ; man, in his essential nature, is divine ; behind the finite man is the Ātman, ever free, ever pure, and ever luminous.

The body, the mind, and the ego are merely the externals of the real man who is immortal and divine. This discovery led to the further discovery that the same divinity is the ground of the world as well. This they termed Brahman, the totality of the Self and the not-Self, which they characterised as *satyaṁ jñānam anantam*—'Truth, Consciousness (or knowledge) and Infinity.'

31. Parā Vidyā and Aparā Vidyā

In the *Muṇḍaka Upaniṣad,* we find this question put by an earnest student to a great teacher (I. I. 3) :

Kasmin nu bhagavo vijñāte sarvam idaṁ vijñātaṁ bhavati—

'What is that reality, O blessed One, by knowing which we can know all that there is in this manifested universe ?'

Is there such a unique reality by knowing which we can understand all the manifestations of nature, internal as well as external ? Is there a unity behind this diversity, a one behind the many ? To this question, the teacher gave a very significant reply (*ibid.*, I. 1.4) :

Dve vidye veditavye, iti ha sma yad brahmavido vadanti, parā caiva aparā ca—

'Two are the *vidyās*, or sciences, to be acquired by man ; so say the knowers of Brahman. One is called *parā vidyā*, higher science or knowledge , the other is called *aparā vidyā*, ordinary science or knowledge.'

Both these must be investigated. Of these, the *aparā* or ordinary knowledge, says the teacher of the Upaniṣad, consists of the sacred Vedas, phonetics, the code of rituals, grammar, etymology, prosody, and astronomy. In fact, it includes, what we would today call, the entire gamut of positivistic knowledge, including the *second-hand* knowledge of the experience of religion, contained in the sacred books of all religions.

Here, we have a scientific mind of the highest order—impersonal, objective, and detached. There is no desire to put forth a pet opinion ; truth alone is the motive power, even if that truth goes against one's pet attachments and aversions. The teacher says that even the Vedas, the sacred books of the whole people, belong to the category of ordinary knowledge. Who would dare to say that his own sacred books are ordinary, except he who is of a detached and scientific frame of mind, and is in search of truth and not a dogma —he who has no truth to hide, no opinion to uphold, no prejudice to defend, who just wants to know the truth and is prepared to sacrifice everything else into the bargain? No religion except that derived from the Upaniṣadic tradition has practised this bold detachment. The follower of every other religion, if asked what is ordinary knowledge, would unhesitatingly reply: All the sacred books of all the religions except my own. But this teacher of the Upaniṣads has the detachment and boldness, proceeding from love of truth, to say that even the Vedas, held in such veneration by himself and by his people, were secondary; all the sacred books and all the positive sciences and the arts are but lower knowledge—*aparā vidyā.*

Sri Ramakrishna, in our time, re-emphasized this spirit when he said: The Vedas and all other sacred books do not contain God, they contain only *information about* God. They are like the Hindu almanac which contains forecast of the rainfall of the year. But, added Sri Ramakrishna, by squeezing the almanac you won't get a drop of water! Similarly, by squeezing the sacred scriptures, none can get God; but by squeezing one's own experience, all can realise God; for He is the one Self of all.

What, then, is left to be included in the category of *parā vidyā*, higher knowledge? The teacher proceeds to indicate this elusive theme. There is a tremendous field of knowledge, area of experience, still left, he thinks ; but it belongs to a different order. So he says (*ibid.*, I. 1.5) :

Atha parā, yayā tad akṣaram
adhigamyate—

'That is *parā vidyā,* or higher science, by which the imperishable (Reality) is realised.'

Physical science and all the rest deal only with things that change, that are perishable. As Sir Arthur Eddington has put it, science gives us 'knowledge of structural form and not knowledge of content'. The sacred books give us, in the words of Sri Ramakrishna referred to above, only *information about* God, and not God Himself. And yet we feel that, in the words of Eddington, 'all through the physical universe runs that unknown content'. What is that content ? And how can we get at it ? If the positive sciences cannot get at it, there must be another discipline, another line of inquiry, which must be able to give us that truth.

If the sacred books contain only information about God, there must be a discipline which gives us God and not merely information about Him. It is this inquiry that pervades the Upaniṣads and that has made them immortal even as literature. And the nature and scope of that inquiry, and the way it was conducted, and the truths gained therefrom, have something superb about them. There is no effort to uphold a mere opinion, however dear ; no struggle to pronounce a dogma and cling to it, and thrust it upon others ; there is no trace of tiredness, or laziness of mind, seeking a resting place on the way. Truth, and nothing but truth, is the watchword. Suffused with the spirit of truth, they declared (*ibid.*, III. 1.6) :

Satyameva jayate nānṛtam,
Satyena panthā vitato devayānaḥ—

'Truth alone triumphs, not untruth ; the path to the luminous Reality is spread out with truth only.'

And this path to the luminous Reality is strewn with the debris of discarded opinions, pleasing dogmas, broken hypotheses, and even dethroned gods ! Thought was not allowed to rest on any of them for long ; it forged ahead on the two wings of *critical discrimination* and *inner detachment, viveka* and *vairāgya,* and wafted by the current of a single-minded passion for truth. One sage puts forth his conclusion about the data of the internal world gathered by him ; another shows it as inadequate ; this stimulates further inquiry, leading to a deeper pronouncement.

There was this unwearied and joyous search, and graceful conflict of thought between the most gifted minds, through which thought forged ahead. There was no national dogma or authoritarian church to suppress or arrest it. The whole process reached its consummation in the profound discovery of the imperishable Self of man, the Ātman, and its spiritual unity with the Self of the universe, the Brahman. The entire process was a joyous voyage of discovery; looking back, they saw that the steps left behind were also valid, and that man travels not from error to truth, but from truth to truth, from lower truth to higher truth.

32. *India's Spiritual Vision of Unity in Diversity*

It is in this context, against this background, that the Indian approach to religion becomes significant. From the time of the Upaniṣads to our own times, India has sought in religion, not a finished dogma to believe in, but a method and a means to pierce the veil that hides the ever-present truth behind man and nature. The Upaniṣads glowingly register this passion of the Indian mind to seek and find truth through a penetrating study of experience. In the appreciative words of the American missionary Robert Ernest Hume (*The Thirteen Principal Upaniṣads,* p. 30, footnote) :

'The earnestness of the search for truth is one of the delightful and commendable features of the Upaniṣads.'

The sages of the Upaniṣads, after a critical and penetrating search into the depth of man—'by means of the subtle *buddhi,* or reason, that had been trained by the sages in the search and discovery of subtle truths', as one of the Upaniṣads puts it—*agryayā buddhyā sūkṣmayā sūkṣmadarśibhiḥ* (*Kaṭha Upaniṣad,* III. 12)—had discovered that imperishable reality as the one and non-dual Self, the Ātman. The opening verse of the *Īśā Upaniṣad* proclaims this sublime truth in a verse which has inspired the philosophy of the *Gītā* and innumerable spiritual seekers thereafter : *Īśāvāsyam idam sarvaṁ yat kiñca jagatyāṁ jagat*—'All this universe, in all its changing forms, is enveloped by the Lord.' The second verse of chapter five of the *Kaṭha Upaniṣad,* which Śaṅkarācārya introduces in his commentary in the words : 'The Ātman is not a dweller in the "city" of one (the human) body only ; what else ? He is the dweller in all bodies', says :

Haṁsaḥ śuciṣat vasu-rantarikṣasat
hotā vediṣat atithir-duroṇasat ;
Nṛṣat varasat ṛtasat vyomasat
abjā gojā ṛtajā adrijā ṛtaṁ bṛhat—

'He is the swan dwelling in the heaven (in the form of the sun), the air filling the atmosphere, the fire dwelling on the altar, the holy guest in the house ; (He is) in man, in gods, in the sacrifice, in the immensity of space ; (He is) born in water (as the aquatic creatures), on the earth (as insects, reptiles and mammals) ; (He is) born as (the fruit of) sacrifice, born of the mountains (as rivers flowing from the mountains to the ocean) ; (He is) the True, the Infinite.'

This great verse, conveying a profound spiritual vision, occurs also in the *Ṛg-Veda* (VI. 40. 5), with the last word omitted. This is the vision that determined the Indian attitude to nature, to the physical, botanical, zoological, and human environments, not as an enemy to be conquered, as in the West, but as a friend to be understood and respected and wisely used. As an enemy, man plunders and ravages nature ; that attitude inevitably passes on to other human beings also, resulting in wars and colonial exploitations and slave trade ; it also produces serious ecological imbalances, until violated nature begins to violate and mutilate the perpetrator himself. This is the tragedy that is being experienced by modern man, and that is posing a serious challenge to human wisdom today.

33. *Sir J. C. Bose and the Scientific Vision of Unity*

The Indian vision of the spiritual unity of all existence is, accordingly, receiving responsive echoes from increasing numbers of thinkers and scientists in the post-war West. Criticisms of economics of affluence, of GNP as the false God of economic growth, of the unbridled pursuit of organic satisfactions, and the ravaging of nature, are increasing in volume and intensity; and books about nature, upholding the Indian vision and quoting Upaniṣadic passages, are coming out in the West more and more. One such recent book is *The Secret Life of Plants* by Peter Tompkins and Christopher Bird, the sub-title of which reads : *Astounding discoveries about the physical, emotional, and spiritual relations between plants and man.* It is a fascinating account of the researches on the subject conducted in the United States, Soviet Russia, and other countries. Concluding their 'Introduction' to the book, the authors say :

'Evidence now supports the vision of the poet and the philosopher that plants are living, breathing, communicating creatures, endowed with personality and the attributes of soul. It is only we, in our blindness, who have insisted on considering them automata.'

What is of special interest to us in India is its chapter 6, entitled 'Plant Life Magnified a Hundred Million Times', containing a moving and vivid account of the pioneering work of the late Sir Jagadish Chandra Bose in this vital field between eight and five decades ago. The authors present, in the opening paragraph, the Bose Institute in Calcutta as the 'Indian Temple of Science' bearing the inscription : 'This temple is dedicated to the feet of God for bringing honour to India and happiness to the world.'

Starting his work of scientific research, initially in the field of physics, in a small twenty-foot-square room for a laboratory, and creating his own tools and instruments, Bose demonstrated the existence and propagation of wireless waves in 1895 in Calcutta. His work in physics led him imperceptibly to botany and physiology, which convinced him of the tenuous nature of the boundary line between 'non-living' metals and 'living' plants and humans, and of the truth of the 'fundamental unity among the apparent diversity of nature'. And on 10th May 1901, he addressed the Royal Institution in London, ending his lecture and experimental demonstration before a mixed, appreciative, sceptical, scientific audience with these words (*The Secret Life of Plants,* pp. 86-87) :

'I have shown you this evening autographic records of the history of stress and strain in the living and non-living. How similar are the writings ! So similar indeed that you cannot tell one apart from the other. Among such phenomena, how can we draw a line of demarcation and say, here the physical ends, and there the physiological begins ? Such absolute barriers do not exist.

'It was when I came upon the mute witness of these self-made records, and perceived in them one phase of a pervading unity that bears within it all things—the mote that quivers in ripples of light, the teeming life upon our earth, and the radiant suns that shine above us—*it was then that I understood, for the first time, a little of that message proclaimed by my ancestors on the banks of the Ganges thirty centuries ago* : "They who see but One, in all the changing manifoldness of this universe, unto them belongs Eternal Truth—unto none else, unto none else".' (italics not by the author).

Giving a sample of the Western reactions to these revolutionary scientific revelations presented by Bose during his trips to Europe in

1919 and 1920, the authors quote, what they term, the 'usually reserved' *Times* of London (*ibid.*, p. 94) :

> 'While we in England were still steeped in the rude empiricism of barbaric life, the subtle Easterner had swept the universe into a synthesis and had seen the *one* in all its changing manifestations.'

The authors conclude the book in these words :

> 'The attraction of the seer's supersensible world, or worlds within worlds, is too great to forego, and the stakes are too high, for they may include survival for the planet. Where the modern scientist is baffled by the secrets of the life of plants, the seer offers solutions which, however incredible, make more sense than the dusty mouthings of academicians ; what is more, they give philosophic meaning to the totality of life.'

34. *Science and Religion Complementary*

Religion expounded as a verified and verifiable science has a message for all humanity. Physical science, through its technology, may build for man a first class house, and equip it with radio, television, and other gadgets ; the social security measures of a modern welfare state may provide him with everything necessary for a happy fulfilled life in this world, and even, through the state church, in the world beyond ; the man himself may give his house such arresting names as Śānti Kuñj (Peace Retreat), or Sukha Vilās (Happy Home). Yet none of these can ensure, by themselves, that he will live in that house in peace or happiness. For that depends, to a large extent, on another source of strength and nourishment, another type of knowledge and discipline—the knowledge and discipline proceeding from the science and technique of religion. If man can have the help of the positive sciences to create a healthy external environment, and the help of the science of spirituality to create a healthy internal environment, he can hope to achieve total life-fulfilment; not otherwise. This is the testament of the Upaniṣads.

But, today, this is not the picture that modern civilisation presents. Man in this technological civilisation is feeling inwardly impoverished and empty in an environment of wealth, power, and pleasure ; he is full of tension and sorrow, doubt and uncertainty, all the time. Juvenile delinquency, drunkenness, suicide, and an increasing variety of other maladies and individual and social distortions, are ever on the increase. Why ? Because man is not inwardly satisfied ; he is smitten with ennui and boredom arising from the limitations of his sense-bound *Weltanschauung*. Indian thinkers foresaw this predicament of modern man ages ago. Says the ancient *Śvetāśvatara Upaniṣad* about the modern space age (VI. 20) :

Yadā carmavad ākāśaṁ
veṣṭayiṣyanti mānavāḥ ;
Tadā devam avijñāya
duḥkhasyānto bhaviṣyati—

'Even though men may (through their technical skill) roll up space like a piece of leather, still there will be no end of sorrow for them without the realisation of the luminous One within.'

Schopenhauer said a hundred years ago (*The World as Will and Idea*, Vol. I. p. 404) :

'All men who are secure from want and care, now that at last they have thrown off all other burdens, become a burden to themselves.'

35. Religion is Realisation

Today, man is his own major burden and problem. He can tackle and solve his problem, not just by going in for more positivistic science, more technology, more life's amenities, more socio-political or micro-biological manipulations of human conditions, but by the cultivation of the science of religion. Says Swami Vivekananda (*Complete Works,* Vol. IV, eighth edition p. 35):

> 'You must bear in mind that religion does not consist in talk, or doctrines, or books, but in realisation; it is not learning, but being.'

It is in this sense that India understood religion; and it is this idea of religion that Swami Vivekananda expounded in the West and the East through his powerful voice. The end and aim of religion, as our ancient teachers put it, is the experience, *anubhava,* of God, through the steady growth in man's spiritual awareness. That is the touchstone of religion. There is such a thing as the *spiritual growth* of the individual, step by step. We experience this growth, just as we see a plant growing, or a building rising up step by step, brick by brick. When we *live* the life of religion, strength comes to us, consciousness becomes expanded, sympathies grow and widen, and we feel that we are growing into better men and women. It is only the strength that proceeds from such inward spiritual growth and development that will enable man to digest and assimilate and discipline the energies released by the progress of scientific technology. Such a man alone has the strength and wisdom to convert the chaos of life into a pattern of peace and happiness and general welfare. If religion is taken away from human society, what remains is simple barbarism. Ancient civilisations were destroyed by barbarians bred outside those civilisations. But modern civilisation, if it is to go the same way, will be destroyed by barbarians bred within the civilisation itself. What can save us from this predicament is a little 'Christian love' in our hearts for our neighbours, in the words of the late Bertrand Russell (*Impact of Science on Society,* p. 114), or a little more altruism, in the words of the late Pitirim S. Sorokin, of Harvard University (*Reconstruction of Humanity,* especially part V). This love comes from the practice of religion, as defined by the world's authentic spiritual teachers. Says Swami Vivekananda, giving a scientific definition of religion (*Complete Works,* Vol. IV, eighth edition, p. 358) :

> 'Religion is the manifestation of the divinity already in man.'

'Now comes the question : Can religion really accomplish anything ?' asked Swami Vivekananda, and proceeded to answer (*ibid.*, Vol. III, eighth edition, p. 4) :

'It can. It brings to man eternal life. It has made man what he is and will make of this human animal a god. That is what religion can do. Take religion from human society and what will remain? Nothing but a forest of brutes. Sense-happiness is not the goal of humanity. Wisdom, *jñāna*, is the goal of all life. We find that man enjoys his intellect more than an animal enjoys its senses; and we see that man enjoys his spiritual nature even more than his rational nature. So the highest wisdom must be this spiritual knowledge. With this knowledge will come bliss.'

36. Significance of Homeostasis in Evolution

Nature has endowed man with the organic capacity to understand the world as well as himself. From the stage of the higher mammals up to man, says biology, as referred to earlier, nature has been developing and perfecting the mechanism of a built-in equilibrium, thermostatic to begin with and homeostatic later, within the organism itself. Dealing with the evolutionary significance of this mechanism, the neurologist Grey Walter says (*The Living Brain*, p. 16):

'The acquisition of internal temperature control, thermostasis, was a supreme event in neural, indeed, in all natural history. It made possible the survival of mammals on a cooling globe. That was its general importance in evolution. Its particular importance was that it completed, in one section of the brain, an automatic system of stabilisation for the vital functions of the organism—a condition known as homeostasis. *With this arrangement, other parts of the brain are left free for functions not immediately related to the vital engine or the senses, for functions surpassing the wonders of homeostasis itself.'* (italics not by the author).

And quoting the significant words, referred to earlier, of physiologist Claude Bernard, that a *fixed interior millieu is the condition for the free life,* Grey Walter continues, (ibid., pp. 16-17) :

'Those who had the privilege of sitting under Sir Joseph Barcroft at Cambridge owe much to him for his explanation of this dictum and its application to physiological research. We might otherwise have been scoffers ; for "the free life" is not a scientific expression. He translated the saying into simple questions and guided us to the answers.

' "What has the organism gained", he asked, "by the constancy of temperature, constancy of hydrogen-ion concentration, constancy of water, constancy of sugar, constancy of oxygen, constancy of calcium, and the rest ?" With his gift for quantitative expression, it was all in the day's work for him to demonstrate the individual intricacies of the various exquisitely balanced feedback mechanisms. But I recall in his manner a kind of modest trepidation, as if he feared we might ridicule his flight of fancy, when he gave us this illustration of homeostasis and its peculiar virtue :

'"How often have I watched the ripples on the surface of a still lake made by a passing boat, noted their regularity and admired the patterns formed when two such ripple-systems meet; ... *but the lake must be perfectly calm*.... To look for high intellectual development in a *milieu* whose properties have not become stabilised, is to seek ... ripple-patterns on the surface of the stormy Atlantic."'

Homeostasis as a fixed interior *milieu* is not an end in itself. It is just a condition, a necessary condition, for life forging ahead to higher and higher evolutionary levels. And the highest level to be reached is the perfect freedom of the human spirit, by detaching the new significant datum of the self from its organic limitations and making it realise its true nature. Nature has achieved *physical* homeostasis for man; man has now to achieve for himself, by himself, through the organic capacities which nature has endowed him with, says Vedānta, a *mental* homeostasis, with a view to realising the Ātman that is behind the mind. After explaining that, through homeostasis, '*the upper brain is freed from the menial tasks of the body, the regulating functions being delegated to the lower brain*', Grey Walter significantly remarks, as referred to earlier, that, for mammals, homeostasis meant only survival; but for man, it points the way to his spiritual freedom.

37. Homeostasis versus Yoga

And relating this physical homeostasis of organic evolution to the mental and spiritual homeostasis of *yoga*, Grey Walter concludes :

'And once again, as new horizons open, we become aware of old landmarks. The experience of homeostasis, the perfect mechanical calm which it allows the brain, has been known for two or three thousand years under various appellations. It is the physiological aspect of all the perfectionist faiths—*nirvāṇa*, the abstraction of the Yogi, the peace that passeth understanding, the derided "happiness that lies within" ; *it is a state of grace in which disorder and disease are mechanical slips and errors.*' (italics not by the author).

The struggle to go beyond organic pulls and limitations, and realise the freedom of the spirit in Self-realisation, needs to be supported and sustained by a stable moral life ; only when this base is secured can man carry forward the struggle directly into the inner world and fashion relevant disciplines, and forge newer instruments out of his psycho-physical energy system, among which a tough *manas* (mind) and a pure *buddhi* (reason and will) are the most important. This results in that second homeostasis, mentioned earlier, which is acquired by man himself with the help of his higher brain after freeing it from thraldom to the organic system. And this second homeostasis is comprehensively called, in Vedānta and Yoga, *sama* and *dama,* discipline of the mind and discipline of the sense organs. This is beautifully brought out in the chariot imagery of the third chapter of the *Kaṭha Upaniṣad,* where *buddhi,* enlightened reason and pure will, is presented as the charioteer of man's journey to freedom and fulfilment.

38. *The Nature of Yoga*

The state in which the mind succeeds in stilling the clamour of the sense organs and itself becomes pure, steady, and still, is called *yoga.* This is the inner condition which spiritual seekers down the ages have striven to attain, and which many have attained, and in which many have realised God, the innermost Self of all, as affirmed by Śrī Kṛṣṇa in the *Gītā* (IV. 10) :

Vīta-rāga-bhaya-krodhā
manmayā mām upāśritāḥ ;
Bahavo jñāna-tapasā
pūtā madbhāvam āgatāḥ—

'Freed from attachment, fear, and anger, absorbed in Me (the one Self in all), and taking refuge in Me, very many people, purified by the *tapas* of *jñāna,* or discipline of spiritual knowledge, have attained to oneness with Me.'

The same truth is affirmed by Gauḍapāda also in his *Māṇḍūkya Upaniṣad Kārikā* (II. 35) :

Vīta-rāga-bhaya-krodhaiḥ
munibhiḥ veda-pāragaiḥ ;
Nirvikalpo hyayaṁ dṛṣṭaḥ
prapañcopaśamo'dvayaḥ—

'This transcendental non-dual state, in which relative existence is overcome, has been attained by sages who were free from attachment, fear, and anger, and who had gone beyond (the mandate of) the Vedas (i.e. of all scriptures, in view of their entering the field of *experiment,* and getting the *experience* of spirituality).'

From the time of the Upaniṣads, about four thousand years ago, and probably even earlier, our country has developed a full-fledged science and technique of this subject, the subject of *yoga.* In the words of Yama in his teaching to the boy Naciketā (*Kaṭha Upaniṣad,* VI. 10-11) :

Yadā pañcāvatiṣṭhante
jñānāni manasā saha ;
Buddhiśca na viceṣṭate

tām āhuḥ paramām gatim.
Tām yogam iti manyante—

'When the five sense organs of knowledge remain steady, along with the *manas,* and even the *buddhi* does not act—that is the supreme state, say (the sages).

'They (the sages) consider that (state) as *yoga.*'

39. *Religion and Science in the Vedāntic Perspective*

Modern civilisation has overrated physical science and technology, just as the older civilisations had underrated it. There is need today to view science in its proper perspective—the perspective of total human knowledge and welfare. This is one of the several vital contributions of Swami Vivekananda to modern thought. Dealing with the complementary character of Eastern contributions to religion and Western contributions to science, he said in his lecture on 'My Master' delivered in New York in 1896 (*Complete Works,* Vol. IV, eighth edition, p. 155) :

'Each of these types has its grandeur, each has its glory. The present adjustment will be the harmonising, the mingling, of these two ideals. To the oriental, the world of spirit is as real as to the occidental is the world of senses. In the spiritual, the oriental finds everything he wants or hopes for; in it, he finds all that makes life real to him. To the occidental, he is a dreamer; to the oriental, the occidental is a dreamer playing with ephemeral toys, and he laughs to think that grown-up men and women should make so much of a handful of matter which they will have to leave sooner or later. Each calls the other a dreamer.

'But the oriental ideal is as necessary for the progress of the human race as is the occidental, and I think it is more necessary. Machines never made mankind happy and never will make. He who is trying to make us believe this will claim that happiness is in the machine; but it is always in the mind. That man alone who is the lord of his mind can become happy, and none else. And what, after all, is this power of machinery? Why should a man who can send a current of electricity through a wire be called a very great man and a very intelligent man? Does not nature do a million times more than that every moment? Why not then fall down and worship nature?'

40. Need for a Synthesis of Science and Religion in Education

Education has to enable all students to achieve at least a fraction of the synthesis of East and West, spirituality and science, contemplation and action. It is the science of spirituality, the *parā-*

vidyā, the supreme science, that fosters in man ethical, aesthetic, and spiritual values, including the moral values associated with pure science. The harmony of all these values, and the intrinsic harmony between science and religion, always upheld in Vedānta, became revealed in our time in the deep spiritual kinship between Narendra (the later Swami Vivekananda), the representative of *aparā-vidyā*, and Sri Ramakrishna, the full embodiment of *parā-vidyā*. All such values emerge from out of the depths of the human spirit at a certain stage of human evolution and after the achievement of some measure of mastery of the environment by him ; they do not emerge from physical nature itself. It is folly, therefore, to believe, or to expect, that they will automatically result from industry or from technological manipulations of physical nature, and from the wealth resulting from such achievements. Protesting against such widely held modern folly, the late Bertrand Russell said (*Impact of Science on Society*, p. 77) :

'The machine as an object of adoration is the modern form of Satan, its worship is the modern diabolism. . . .

'Whatever else may be mechanical, values are not, and this is something which no political philosopher must forget.'

It is thus obvious that, if the current secular school and university education is high and higher education, the spiritual education that Swami Vivekananda received from Sri Ramakrishna in our time, bearing wonderful fruits of character-strength and compassion, deep as the ocean and broad as the skies, and harmonising East and West, religion and science, the sacred and the secular, is the highest education into which the other two, to fulfil themselves, must lead a child. Sri Ramakrishna's experience and example also make it clear that man can enter into, and benefit from, this spiritual education from any stage or level of his school or college education. Wisdom can accompany, and enliven, and creatively stimulate, knowledge at any level—primary or secondary, under-graduate or post-graduate. It is also equally clear that, without a little of that wisdom, knowledge at any of these levels can become, in the long run, not a blessing but a curse to oneself and to society, a breeding ground of pride, selfishness, exploitation, and violence, on the one hand, and alienation, loneliness, and psychic breakdowns, on the other. These have afflicted societies and civilisations in the past, and led them to decay and death. And modern Western civilisation is also facing that challenge today. As our own country also is absorbing the energies of this modern civilisation at a fast pace today, and is already experiencing some of its distortions, we shall be wise if we open ourselves up also to the eternal message of our *adhyātmavidyā*, or science of man in depth, and generate a fresh capital of our spiritual energy resources, with a view to digesting, assimilating, and transforming the physical and mental energy resources of our highly technical age.

41. Vastu-tantra-jñāna versus Puruṣa-tantra-jñāna

The modern age demands that we meet the challenges of life with the challenge of an adequate philosophy ; that adequacy can be ensured only if that philosophy dares to achieve a happy synthesis between the physical sciences and the science of spirituality. And this is the speciality of our Vedānta among the passing philosophies of the world. Vedānta is the only philosophy that is not only unafraid of the advance of scientific knowledge, but also warmly welcomes it. Truth is its passion—*satyameva jayate*—and not any pleasing opinion or dogma. Like modern physical science, Vedānta fosters the critical inquiring spirit, along with detachment, objectivity, precision, and the challenge of verification. No field of knowledge can foster these moral and intellectual virtues and graces, unless it is on the track of objective truth, and not of mere personal subjective fancies and satisfactions.

This scientific characteristic of Vedānta is boldly brought out by Śaṅkarācārya, while presenting the great theme of *Brahma-jijñāsā*, or inquiry into Brahman, in his commentary on the *Brahma-sūtra*, and while expounding the scientific frame of mind in his commentary on the *Gītā*. In the former, he makes a distinction between *vastu-tantra-jñāna,* knowledge depending on, and arising from, the *vastu* or existing reality, and *puruṣa-tantra-jñāna,* knowledge depending on the *puruṣa,* the person, on the moods and fancies and interests of the person concerned. *Vastu-tantra-jñāna,* being knowledge of an existing fact, is independent of the knowing person ; that knowledge is only the discovery of the fact, but it does not create it ; whereas *puruṣa-tantra-jñāna* is knowledge dependent on the person, and is, accordingly, susceptible of being held, altered, or abolished, depending on the person concerned—*kartum, akartum, anyathā-kartuṁ śakyate, puruṣa-tantratvāt eva,* as observed by Śaṅkarācārya.

There is a vast field of human preferences constituting such *puruṣa-tantra* knowledge, and they have their legitimate role to play in human life. But God and soul, as understood in Vedānta, are not mere subjective fancies, but belong to the field of *vastu-tantra* inquiry and knowledge; 'Brahman, immediate and direct, which is the innermost Self of all', as we have earlier heard the *Bṛhadāraṇyaka Upaniṣad* describing the truth of God. Brahman as the Self of all, as the *pratyagātman,* is the only rational sanction for ethics and morality. It is an ever-present Reality, as the knower behind all acts of perception and knowledge, who cannot be made an *object* of knowledge, but yet whose negation also is an impossibility; for, He or It is the very Self of him who does the negation: *ya eva nirākartā tasyaiva ātmatvāt.* This Brahman is not any extra-cosmic deity of the usual run of monotheism, which is only a logical postulate equally capable of being enthroned or dethroned by human reason, or merely held by faith but is not capable of verification. But the Brahman of the Upaniṣads, being the one Self of all, is the very basis and consummation of experience—*anubhavāvasānatvāt bhūta-vastu-viṣayatvāt ca brahma-jñānasya*—'because the knowledge of Brahman is consummated in experience and refers, therefore, to an existing *vastu,* or fact.' It is unknown, in the state of spiritual ignorance, but it is not unknowable ; for it is the very Self of the knower and, hence, is more intimately known than any sense object. But this knowledge is obstructed and obscured by the self-not-self mix-up in normal experience, calling for a discriminative inquiry.

The sages of the Upaniṣads realised, through such a penetrating inquiry and search, this infinite and immortal Ātman in themselves, behind the five ever-changing *kośas,* or sheaths, of the body, the nervous system, the mind, the intellect, and the bliss of egolessness. Says Yama, the teacher, to Naciketā, the young student (*Kaṭha Upaniṣad*, III. 12) :

Eṣa sarveṣu bhūteṣu
gūḍho ātmā na prakāśate ;
Dṛśyate tvagryayā buddhyā
sūkṣmayā sūkṣma-darśibhiḥ—

'This Ātman, (being) hidden in all beings, is not manifest to all. But it *can be realised* by all who are trained to inquire into subtle truths, by means of their sharp and subtle *buddhi* or pure Reason.'

We get an echo of this concept of the sheaths covering reality in twentieth-century biology, with respect to the first three, including the *Taittirīya Upaniṣad* emphasis of 'infilling of the succeeding by the preceding' : *tenaiṣa pūrṇaḥ*—'this is infilled by that'. Says the American biologist George Gaylord Simpson (*The Meaning of Evolution,* p. 312) :

'A broad classification of the sciences into physical, biological, and social corresponds with three levels of organisation of matter and energy, and not levels only, but also quite distinct kinds of organisation. The three are sharply increasing orders of complexity, and each includes the lower grades. Vital organisation is more intricate than physical organisation, and it is added to and does not replace physical organisation, which is also fully involved in vital organisation. Social organisation retains and sums the complexities of both these and adds its own still greater complexities.'

The impurities of the mind constitute the obstructions to the knowledge of this ever-present divine immortal dimension of man. These impurities are centred in the ego, in its attachments and aversions and bondage to the organic system. Search for truth, either in the external world which yields scientific knowledge, or in the internal world which yields spiritual experience, calls for the elimination of these impurities which alone gives the mind the power to penetrate from the surface to the depths of nature, external or internal. This is the scientific spirit and temper which is highlighted in Śrī Kṛṣṇa's exhortation to Arjuna in the *Gītā*, and which is amplified in Śaṅkarācārya's commentary on the same (VII. 27-28) :

Icchā-dveṣa-samuthena
dvandva-mohena bhārata ;
Sarvabhūtāni saṁmoham
sarge yānti parantapa—

'By the delusion of the pairs of opposites arising from attachment and aversion, O descendant of Bharata, all beings are fallen into deep delusion at birth, O scorcher of foes.'

Yeṣāṁ tvantagataṁ pāpam
janānāṁ puṇya-karmaṇām ;
Te dvandva-moha-nirmuktāḥ
bhajante māṁ dṛḍhavratāḥ—

'But those men of virtuous deeds whose impurities have been destroyed—they, freed from all the delusions of the pairs of opposites, worship Me with firm resolve.'

Commenting on the first, Śaṅkarācārya observes :

'For it is well known that knowledge of *things as they are,* even in the external world, cannot rise in the minds of those who are under the thraldom of attachment and aversion ; if this is so, what wonder is there that knowledge of the inner Self, which is faced with many obstacles, does not arise in those who are enslaved by them and consequently are deeply deluded ! Hence all beings, *whose reason is obstructed and deeply deluded* by the delusion of these pairs of opposites, do not know Me, who am their very Self, and, hence also, they do not worship Me as their own Self.'

42. *Science and Religion versus Magic and Miracles*

Some of our people, especially among our educated sections, including our administrative personnel, run after all sorts of magic and miracles, puerile and sterile, in the name of religion and *yoga.* In this age of the marvels of physical science, *such religious magic and miracles appear infantile.* What magic and miracles, performed in the name of a cheap religion and *yoga,* and held in secret by the performers, can compare with the 'miracles' performed by the physical sciences, *verified* and *verifiable, open* and *communicable,* whether in the field of curing of diseases, and that too, on a mass scale, *increasing of food production*, or putting a man or a vehicle on the Moon or the Mars and bringing both back to earth !

The great Buddha discouraged all miracles and secrecy in religion. What is secret may not be sacred. What is sacred need not be secret. His teachings were profound, but were open, *ehi passa, ehi passa*, 'come and see, come and see', as he picturesquely expressed it. Addressing his disciple Ānanda, he said : The Tathāgata has no secrecy ; secrecy belongs to three things, O Ānanda : to priestly knowledge, to false knowledge, and to prostitutes.

It is imperative that our people turn away from the cheap and *secret* miracles of *yoga* and religion, indulgence in which had kept our people weak and superstitious and in political slavery for centuries, and turn to master the marvellous and beneficial and *open* 'miracles' of physical science for our individual and collective welfare.

The only 'miracle' that can match, *and also over-match*, the great miracles of modern physical sciences is the 'miracle' of character produced by pure religion, by the science of spirituality. Purity, love, compassion, work-efficiency, dedication, and service—these are the wonderful fruits which are produced by the science of religion in us. Gandhiji wrought, and taught, the miracles of transmuting hatred into love and violence into non-violence.

Dependence on the cheap miracles of religion and *yoga* weakens the human mind ; *they are hypnotic in their effects.* Vedānta and all the great spiritual teachers of the world, therefore, always discouraged them. Vivekananda preached Vedānta to *de-hypnotise* such and other already hypnotised people in the East and the West ; 'Strength, strength, is what the Upaniṣads preach to me from every page', he proclaimed. He preferred people becoming atheistic and agnostic to becoming superstitious fools ; for the atheist and the agnostic, he said, can still attain freedom, but not those who are weakened by superstition. That is why Śrī Kṛṣṇa preached, in the *Gītā*, *buddhiyoga,* the *yoga* of Reason, as the unfailing guide in life.

Vedānta has provided the science of religion with an intelligible and international framework of terms and concepts, which help the various religions of the world to understand themselves, to understand and welcome each other, and to understand and appreciate the physical sciences. This is precisely the service that modern physical science has rendered to all physical or positivistic knowledge. Both thus become, though developed in different countries and in different periods of history, human contributions to knowledge and life fulfilment. In the *Gītā*, Śrī Kṛṣṇa describes the 'without' of nature as the aspect of *aparā prakṛti,* or ordinary nature and the 'within' of nature as the aspect of *parā prakṛti,* or higher nature, of the one total divine Nature (VII. 5) :

> *Apareyam itastvanyām*
> *prakṛtiṁ viddhi me parām ;*
> *Jīva-bhūtāṁ mahābāho*
> *yayedaṁ dhāryate jagat—*

'This is (My) ordinary nature ; but, other than this, know My higher nature, O mighty-armed (Arjuna), which is of the nature of Intelligence and by which this whole universe is sustained.'

Commenting on this statement of Srī Krsna in his comment on the next verse, verse 6, Śaṅkarācārya says :

> *Prakṛti-dvaya-dvāreṇa ahaṁ*
> *sarvajña īśvaro jagataḥ kāraṇam—*

'Through this twofold Nature, I, who am God the all-knowing (being of the nature of pure Consciousness), am the cause of this universe.'

The combination of these two, namely, religion, or the scientific approach to the 'within' of nature, and modern science, or the scientific approach to the 'without' of nature, constitutes *the complete education for fulfilment* for all humanity today. Echoing this conviction in the concluding portion of his *Autobiography*, astrophysicist R. A. Millikan says :

'It seems to me that the two great pillars upon which all human well-being and human progress rest are first, the spirit of religion, and second, the spirit of science—or knowledge. Neither can attain its largest effectiveness without support from the other. To promote the latter we have universities and research institutions. *But the supreme opportunity for everyone with no exception lies in the first.*' (italics not by the author).

43. *Rationalism and the March of Reason*

I have discussed earlier the limitations of physical science as well as the limitations of dogma-bound religion, and have referred to Swami Vivekananda's strong plea to subject religion to rational scrutiny. In the wake of the materialistic world-picture of nineteenth-century science, religion came under the attack of not only physical science, but also of a philosophy and of a movement known as rationalism, which has done good work to encourage clear thinking. But post-war rationalists and rationalism have become somewhat anachronistic by continuing to swear by a physical science which is now no more what it was in the last century. The humility of twentieth-century science is yet to invade the citadel of that rationalism. That wholesome invasion will be accomplished when rationalism recognises the distinction between religion, on the one side, and superstition and obscurantism, on the other. But, today, its fight against all religion, in the absence of this recognition, has itself become an irrational venture. It can overcome this irrationality only when it grasps the limitations of the reason it handles, *and recognises the truth of the march of reason.* It will then find all the forces of religion also on its side in its fight against all superstition and obscurantism.

What is the meaning of the statement that logical reason, which is the instrument of logic and scientific method, is limited in scope and feels baffled by the mystery of the external universe? Logical reason is inconclusive—*tarka-apratiṣṭhānāt*—is also a famous statement of the *Brahma-sūtra* of Bādarāyaṇa. Reason is a precious value thrown up by evolution and the source of much human progress in culture and civilisation. The discovery of its inadequacy is itself the fruit of man's insatiable love of truth, and his passion to push forward in its search. *The discovery of the limitations of reason, therefore, is not, and should not be allowed to become, a signal to revert to unreason or less reason.* It has to be further developed into a more adequate instrument for pursuing the quest for truth. This is what Vedānta achieved in its *buddhi,* or philosophical Reason, as I have discussed earlier. This is conveyed in a lucid utterance of Swami Vivekananda (*Complete Works,* Vol. I, eleventh edition, p. 185):

> 'On reason we must have to lay our foundation; we must follow reason as far as it leads; and when reason fails, reason itself will show us the way to the highest plane.'

Vedānta sees the chief basis of this limitation of scientific reason in its sole dependence on the observed sense data of the external world and neglect of the observer or experiencer of the inner world. Within the field of sense experience, scientific reason is the most versatile instrument of knowledge of truth. Man has, by slow degrees, developed this instrument, along with its most important tool, namely, language, in precision and range, and has successfully dealt with the baffling and confused mass of data pouring in upon him from his external world. With these great achievements to its credit, how can anyone speak with finality about the limitations of human reason? Have we not seen reason's limitations being overcome by reason itself in the brief course of human history? What a distance has reason travelled, from an uncertain tool in the hands of primitive man to an efficient instrument in the hands of twentieth-century scientist! Can we not expect, therefore, that reason itself will overcome whatever limitations have come into view in its scope and function?

The answer of Vedānta to these doubts and questionings is bold and clear and positive; and behind that answer lies an impressive record of human endeavour, as I have shown earlier, to develop human reason and human language as instruments to secure for man satisfaction in his insatiable hunger for truth, for knowledge for its own sake, and, to a lesser extent, in his search for general human happiness and welfare. Vedānta holds that reason is the most precious possession of man and that it should be kept bright and pure, and that nothing should be indulged in which weakens or destroys it.

The truth of the march of reason is revealed in the history of reason's confrontation with experience, with deeper and deeper layers of experience. Reason as experienced in formal logic is under the most rigid framework, and has very little to do with experience. And this fact explains its static and formal nature and its incapacity to give new knowledge. In all formal logical deductions, the conclusion is only the re-statement of the proposition itself. Reason achieves a direct confrontation with experience in the logic of scientific method. It was this discipline of experience that enabled scientific inductive reason, with the help of disciplined deduction, to achieve its great successes from the seventeenth to the nineteenth century, in unravelling the mysteries of external nature. But, by the end of the nineteenth century, scientific reason also, in the field of physics, began to feel even the erstwhile framework of classical physics too rigid for its expansive mood. Says physicist the late Heisenberg (*Physics and Philosophy*, p. 169):

'The nineteenth century developed an extremely rigid frame for natural science, which formed not only science, but also the general outlook of great masses of people. This frame was supported by the fundamental concepts of classical physics, space, time, matter, and causality; the concept of reality applied to the things or events that we could perceive by our senses or that could be observed by means of the refined tools that technical science had provided. Matter was the primary reality. The progress of science was pictured as a crusade of conquest into the material world. Utility was the watchword of the time. . . This frame was so narrow and rigid that it was difficult to find a place in it for many concepts of our language that had always belonged to its very substance, for instance, the concepts of mind, of the human soul, or of life.'

The breakdown of this rigid framework of classical physics, and of its reason, became inevitable at the end of the nineteenth century with the discovery of a mass of new facts regarding the physical world, more especially of the sub-atomic world. The development of the quantum and relativity theories accelerated this process through the early decades of the present century, until the old framework became utterly untenable. The most revolutionary aspect of this change lay in repudiating the exclusively 'objective' character of the so-called objective world studied by science, and the consequent change in its concept of reality. Pointing out the significance of the quantum theory in this connection, Heisenberg says (*ibid.*, p. 33):

'It is in the quantum theory that the most fundamental changes with respect to the concept of reality have taken place, and in quantum theory in its final form the new ideas of atomic physics are concentrated and crystallised. . . .*But the change in the concept of reality manifesting itself in quantum theory is not simply a continuation of the past; it seems to be a real break in the structure of modern science.'* (italics not by the author).

The history of modern science reveals the distance travelled by reason from the sterility of formal logic, through the fruitful, though rigid, framework of classical physics, to the revolutionary and expansive heights of quantum and relativity physics. *Every advance in the march of reason, every step forward in achieving reason's clarity and effectiveness, has been the product of increase in detachment, in subtlety, and in the range of facts.* The reason of formal logic rose beyond its own limitations by developing into the reason of classical physics with its stress on induction and verification ; the reason of classical physics similarly transcended its own limitations by growing into the reason of twentieth-century physics.

In this latest development, reason has achieved an evaluation of experience, and a criticism of itself, far surpassing anything that was ever achieved in the whole range of Western thought, scientific or philosophical. It is obvious that neither the reason of formal logic nor the reason of classical physics, which is the reason handled by rationalists and their rationalism, can handle the values that lie beyond the sensate level. For, that reason, as shown by modern depth psychology, is a fugitive in the hands of the unconscious and the sub-conscious. Their limitations proceed from what Sir James Jeans calls their 'purely human angle of vision'. Vedānta expresses the same idea by saying that *their limitations proceed from their confining themselves to the data of the waking, or jāgrat, state only.* In quantum and relativity physics, as also in other branches of science like twentieth-century biology and Freudian psychology, reason has broken through this rigid framework of the waking state, with its sense data and the ego, its synthetic *a priori* concepts, its limited ideas of subject and object, its notion of substantiality as the criterion of reality, and copy, correspondence, and coherence, etc. as criteria of truth. It has thus released reason from its sensate tether, or to use the Vedāntic language, from its *waking-state* tether, and set it on the high road of adventure into the mystery of the unknown in man and nature, through the study, in Vedāntic terminology, of the data of the waking and dream states in correlation.

The reality that confronts reason in twentieth-century physics is not static *objects* in space and time, but dynamic *events* in a space-time continuum, in which all objects and subjects of the waking state become just passing *configurations* of that space-time. It is significant to note that it is this dimension of experience that is revealed in the dream state. If science finds that the subject or observer enters into its knowledge of the objective world, and if the purely objective is nowhere to be found—and this is the situation in nuclear physics—it will be only true to itself if it enters into an inquiry into the unique datum of the subject, or the observer, or the self, with a view to investigating the reality underlying all events or phenomena. With this widening of the field of investigation, the development and sharpening of reason has also to keep pace, in order to make it subtler and subtler, clearer and clearer, to cope with the subtler and subtler dimensions of reality. This is achieved through greater and greater intellectual detachment and moral purity, arising from the liberation of reason, according to Vedānta, from thraldom to man's sensate nature.

When this is done, the logic of the conscious and the logic of the unconscious, the logic of the waking state and the logic of the dream state, become fused into the grand logic of all *dṛśyam*, or the totality of all percepts and concepts. The reason that comprehends this grand sweep of all *dṛśyam* is the *buddhi* of Vedānta, which alone has the capacity to turn its searchlight on the *dṛk,* or subject, or seer, or observer, behind all *dṛśyam.* The answer to the question, what is the 'known'? cannot be found until the answer to the question, who is the 'knower'? is found. Scientific reason has already established the relative character of all objects experienced in the waking state, as also of its ideas of time, space, and causality. As configurations of the space-time continuum, these had been interpreted by relativity physics as possessing some reality which, in their separate forms, was denied to them. The study of dream similarly reveals the unreality of the separate dream presentations and the reality of the *citta* or mind-stuff. It is this investigation, and its further pursuit, says Vedānta, that opens the way to developing scientific reason into *buddhi,* or philosophical Reason.

Philosophical Reason not only discovers the relativity, finitude and changeability of all *dṛśyam,* including the egos of the waking and dream states, but it also asks the fundamental philosophical question whether there is a changeless reality somewhere in the depth of experience, and if there is such a reality, what is its nature and what is its relation to the entire world of the *dṛśyam.* Knowledge and memory are data which demand the unity and unchangeability of the knowing subject or the self; but the egos of the waking and dream states are changeable and mutually exclusive.

Does experience disclose a changeless subject beyond the egos of the two states ? For seeking an answer to this vital question, Vedāntic reason finds it necessary to investigate the philosophical significance of the third state, or *avasthā,* apart from the two, waking and dream, namely, *suṣupti,* or dreamless sleep, in which all the subjects and objects of the other two states disappear and merge in the one eternal subject, of the nature of pure Consciousness, the Ātman or Brahman, and of which the whole world of presentations, with their subjects and objects, are but passing configurations. Vedānta insists that this insight into what *suṣupti* reveals comes to reason only when it becomes pure by shedding its last and persistent attachment, namely, the causal notion of the waking state, a notion, which, even in the waking state, is found to be untenable by quantum physics. The Reality that then shines is described by Vedānta as the *turīya,* which the *Māṇḍūkya Upaniṣad,* in its verse 7, describes as :

Adṛśyam, avyavahāryam, agrāhyam, alakṣaṇam, acintyam, avyapadeśyam, ekātmapratyayasāram, prapañcopaśamam, śāntam, śivam, advaitam, caturtham manyante—sa ātmā sa vijñeyaḥ—

'Unseen, not caught in the network of relativity,

ungrasped (by speech and all other sense organs), without any indicating marks (which alone makes logical inference possible), ungrasped by thought, without any name (for identification), of the essence of the consciousness of the unity of the Self, the tranquillisation of the ever-changing world phenomena, (all) peace, goodness, and non-duality—that is considered as the Fourth—He is the Ātman ; He is to be realised.'

The Ātman is thus the unity of all experience ; this entire universe is the Ātman, which is of the nature of *cit,* or pure Consciousness. Being the Self of all, Ātman is *cit-svarūpam* and *advitīyam,* 'of the very nature of pure Consciousness', and 'infinite and non-dual.' Says the nuclear physicist Erwing Schrodinger on the nature of consciousness (*What is Life*? pp. 90-91):

> Consciousness is never experienced in the plural, only in the singular.... Consciousness is a singular of which the plural is unknown ; that there is only one thing and that, what seems to be a plurality, is merely a series of different aspects of this one thing, produced by a deception (the Indian *Māyā*).'

It was this *lokottara,* (i.e., transcendental, beyond cause) Consciousness that the great Buddha realised on that blessed full moon night over 2,500 years ago. Referring to this realisation, he told his disciples later : (*Sūtta Pīṭaka, Majjhima Nikāya, Sūtta* 26 : *Ariya-pariyeṣaṇa Sūtta*) :

'I attained the supreme peace of an ego-extinction not affected by decay, ... disease, ... death, ... grief, ... and defilement. And the *jñānam*, or Knowledge, now as a thing seen (*darśanam*) arose in me: My *vimukti*, or liberation, is established : *jāti*, or subjection to the causal chain, is terminated here (in this birth) ; there is not now *punarbhava*, or re-birth.'

And, again :

'Hearken, monks, the *amṛtam*, or the Immortal, has been gained by me. I teach, I show the Truth.'

In the course of another discourse in the Jeta grove of Śrāvasti, Buddha uttered these solemn words clarifying the *nirvāṇa* experience of this *lokottara*, or *turīya*, state (*Udāna*, Woodward's translation) :

'There is, brethren, an unborn, a not-become, a not-made, a not-compounded. If there were not, brethren, this that is unborn, not become, not made, not compounded, there could not be made any escape from what is born, become, made, compounded.

'But since, brethren, there is this unborn, not-become, not-made, not-compounded, therefore is there made known an escape from what is born, become, made, compounded.'

In his *Māṇḍūkyo'paniṣad Kārikā,*Gauḍapāda refers to Brahman as pure Consciousness and as above causality (III. 33) :

Akalpakam ajaṁ jñānam
jñeyābhinnaṁ pracakṣate ;
Brahma jñeyam ajaṁ nityam
ajenā-jaṁ vibudhyate—

The *jñānam*, i.e. reason or knowledge, which is beyond causality, and free from all conceptual limitations, is ever inseparable from the knowable (Reality). Brahman is the sole knowable (Reality), eternal and beyond causality. The unborn or the non-causal (Brahman) is realized by the unborn or the non-causal (reason or knowledge).'

And, giving his obeisance to the human guru who has realised the highest truth (of the unity of all experience as the Self), which is beyond all cause and effect relations, Gauḍapāda says (*ibid.*, IV. 1) :

Jñānenākāśa-kalpena
dharmān yo gaganopamān ;
Jñeyābhinnena saṁbuddhaḥ
taṁ vande dvipadāṁ varam—

'I bow down to that best among human beings who, with his *jñāna,* reason or knowledge, which (as pure Consciousness) is (infinite) like the void, has realised the non-separateness of the objects and entities of the universe, which are also (infinite) like the Void, from the Knowable (i.e. Brahman).'

In the words of Sri Ramakrishna:

'*Śuddha manas,* or pure mind, *śuddha* buddhi, or pure reason, and *śuddha Ātman,* or pure Self, are one and the same Reality.'

The Bṛhadāraṇyaka Upaniṣad, in a majestic passage, describes the *prāṇas*, or the energies of the world, as *satyam*, or truth, and presents the Ātman as *satyasya satyam,* or the Truth of truth (II. i. 20):

Sa yathorṇanābhiḥ tantunoccaret,
yathāgneḥ kṣudrā visphuliṅgā vyuccaranti;
Evam eva asmāt ātmanaḥ
sarve prāṇāḥ, sarve lokāḥ,
sarve devāḥ, sarvāṇi bhūtāni, vyuccaranti.
Tasyo'paniṣat—satyasya satyamiti;
prāṇā vai satyam, teṣām eṣa satyam—

'As a spider moves along the thread (of the web produced by it from itself), and as from a (blazing) fire, tiny sparks fly in all directions, so from this Ātman emanate all energies, all worlds, all *devas* (luminous beings), and all entities. Its mystical name is—"the Truth of truth". The cosmic energies (of the world) are truth; and This is the Truth of those (energies).'

The *Śrīmad Bhāgavatam* (I. ii. 11) refers to the *tattva-vidaḥ,* i.e. the knowers of Truth, who present the *tattvam,* or Truth, as *advayaṁ jñānam*, non-dual *jñānam*, i.e. pure Knowledge or Reason or Consciousness or Experience-field.

The scientific method which reason pursues to realise this ever-present unity is described by Vedānta as the *avasthā-traya-prakriyā*—the methodology of the three *avasthās,* or states. This is reason comprehending all reality, external and internal, objective and subjective, the 'without' and the 'within' of all nature.

It is because of the very limited nature of the reason of rationalism that it is unable to distinguish between spirituality and superstition and, with a sense of cock-sureness, fights with both; and it is because reason in twentieth-century science has become expansive that it stands in reverence before the great mystery of the unknown and is drawn towards it irresistibly.

Reason that sunders reality into scientific, artistic, and religious fields shows only its own limitation, and not of reality; such separation is permissible, as in the case of the different names of the one ocean surrounding the earth, as a provisional approach for purposes of study and analysis ; but, if pursued too far, and treated as final, it distorts reality. It is the supreme function of philosophical Reason, says Vedānta, to synthesise the conclusions of the various branches of human knowledge and experience and achieve a vision of the total and integral reality. Reason in Vedānta achieved this comprehensive vision of reality and discovered thereby the ever-present harmony, not only between religion and religion, but also between religion, art, and physical science. The Vedāntic vision of unity became, accordingly, the meeting ground of faith and reason, love and knowledge, poetry and philosophy, art and science. Referring to this sweep of the *buddhi,* or philosophical Reason, of Vedānta, as presented by Swami Vivekananda in the modern age, Sister Nivedita writes (*Complete Works*, Vol. I, eleventh edition, Introduction, pp. xiii-xiv) :

'To him, there is no difference between service of man and worship of God, between manliness and faith, between true righteousness and spirituality. All his words, from one point of view, read as a commentary upon this central conviction : "Art, Science, and Religion", he said once, "are but three different ways of expressing a single truth. But in order to understand this, we must have the theory of *advaita* (non-duality)." '

44. Modern Physics and Philosophical Reason

In countless ways, every department of physical science today is extending the bounds of man's knowledge of fundamental unity behind the manifold diversities of the universe. Physical science started with the exploration of the mysteries of external nature ; but at the farthest end of this search, it finds itself face to face with the mystery of man, of his mind and consciousness, the deepest mystery of all. The philosophies of the East, particularly the Vedãnta of India, including Buddhist thought, directly faced this mystery of man, more than two thousand years ago, by initiating the exploration of the internal world and carrying it through to its depths. And, today, we witness a steady convergence of these two indirect and direct approaches in the steady emergence of a common philosophy of the one behind the many.

Physicists of the first quarter of this century, faced with the challenge of the revolutionary discoveries of relativity and quantum physics, turned into bold philosophical thinkers, initiating the development of reason of physics into *buddhi* or philosophical Reason, by transforming it into a critique, not only of the observed sense data of the physical world, but also of man the observer. Starting with Eddington, Jeans, Max Planck, Einstein, Shrodinger, Niels Bohr, Heisenberg, and other great creators of twentieth-century physics, this philosophical trend has grown through the last five decades, culminating, about three years ago, in *The Tao of Physics* of Berkeley University Physics Professor, Dr. Fritjof Capra.

Concluding his *Space, Time, and Gravitation,* Eddington hinted at the emergence of the mystery of man from the study of the mystery of physical nature :

'The theory of relativity has passed in review the whole subject-matter of physics. It has unified the great laws which, by the precision of their formulation and the exactness of their application, have won the proud place in human knowledge which physical science holds today. And yet, in regard to the nature of things, this knowledge is only an empty shell—a form of symbols. *It is knowledge of structural form, and not knowledge of content.* All through the physical world runs that unknown content, *which must surely be the stuff of our consciousness.* Here is a hint of aspects deep within the world of physics, and yet unattainable by the methods of physics. And, moreover, we have found that, where science has progressed the farthest, *the mind has but regained from nature that which the mind has put into nature. We have found a strange footprint on the shores of the unknown. We have devised profound theories, one after another, to account for its origin. At last, we have succeeded in reconstructing the creature that made the footprint. And lo! it is our own.'* (italics not by the author).

Hints such as these, given by the earlier philosopher-scientists, have developed into positive affirmations in Dr. Capra of this decade. The very title of his book: *The Tao of Physics,* is significant in this connection, apart from the masterly and fascinating exposition he gives, in the course of the book, of his main thesis that:

'the basic elements of the Eastern world-view are also those of the world-view emerging from modern physics',

and that

'Eastern thought, and more generally, mystical thought, provide a consistent and relevant philosophical background to the theories of contemporary science.' (*The Tao of Physics,* p. 25).

Noting that, through the two centuries of association with the philosophy of materialism and mechanism, and the contemporary reactions against the ravages wrought by over-technology, the image of science in the eyes of modern man has suffered much damage, Capra seeks to restore the image of pure science as the discipline in the pursuit of truth and human excellence, not in opposition, but in tune, with the spiritual heritage of man, and more especially, of the spiritual heritage of the East (*ibid.*) :

> 'This book aims at improving the image of science by showing that there is an essential harmony between the spirit of Eastern wisdom and Western science. *It attempts to suggest that modern physics goes far beyond technology, that the way—or Tao—of physics can be a path with a heart, a way to spiritual knowledge and self-realisation.*'

Echoing the voice of Vedānta and all mystical thought that the fundamental search for reality takes man beyond the senses and the sensory world of phenomena, Capra says (*ibid.*, p. 51) :

> 'On this journey to the world of the infinitely small, the most important step, from a philosophical point of view, was the first one : the step into the world of atoms. Probing inside the atom and investigating its structure, science transcended the limits of our sensory imagination. From this point on, it could no longer rely with absolute certainty on logic and commonsense. Atomic physics provided the scientists with the first glimpses of the essential nature of things. Like the mystics, *physicists were now dealing with a non-sensory experience of reality* and, like the mystics, they had to face the paradoxical aspects of this experience.

From then on, therefore, the models and images of modern physics became akin to those of Eastern philosophy.'

Referring to the basic unity of the universe, as upheld in Eastern mysticism and modern physics, Capra says (*ibid.*, pp. 130-31) :

'The most important characteristic of the Eastern world-view—one could almost say the essence of it—is the awareness of the unity and mutual interrelation of all things and events. ... The Eastern traditions constantly refer to this ultimate indivisible reality, which manifests itself in all things, and of which all things are parts. It is called *Brahman* in Hinduism, *Dharmakāya* in Buddhism, *Tao* in Taoism. . . .

'The basic oneness of the universe is not only the central characteristic of the mystical experience, but is also one of the most important revelations of modern physics. It becomes apparent at the atomic level, and manifests itself more and more as one penetrates deeper into matter, down into the realm of sub-atomic particles. *The unity of all things and events will be a recurring theme throughout our comparison of modern physics and Eastern philosophy.*'

Both speak of reality as transcending space, time, and causality. Referring to this kinship, Dr. Capra says (*ibid.*, pp. 186-87) :

'The space-time of relativistic physics is a similar timeless space of a higher dimension. All events in it are interconnected, but the connections are not causal. Particle interactions can be interpreted in terms of cause and effect only when the space-time diagrams are read in a definite direction, e.g. from the bottom to the top. When they are taken as four dimensional patterns without any definite direction of time attached to them, there is no "before" and no "after", and thus no causation.

'Similarly, the Eastern mystics assert that, in transcending time, they also transcend the world of cause and effect. Like our ordinary notions of space and time, causation is an idea which is limited to a certain experience of the world and has to be abandoned when this experience is extended. In the words of Swami Vivekananda (*Jñāna Yoga*, p. 169):

' "Time, space, and causation are like the glass through which the Absolute is seen. . . . In the Absolute there is neither time, space, nor causation."

'The Eastern spiritual traditions show their followers various ways of going beyond the ordinary experience of time and of freeing themselves from the chain of cause and effect—from the bondage of *karma*, as the Hindus and Buddhists say. It has therefore been said that Eastern mysticism is a liberation from time. The same may be said of relativistic physics.'

Again (*ibid.*, p. 211):

'Subsequent to the emergence of the field concept, physicists have attempted to unify the various fields into a single fundamental field which would incorporate all physical phenomena. Einstein, in particular, spent the last years of his life searching for such a unified field. The *Brahman* of the Hindus, like the *Dharmakāya* of the Buddhists, and the *Tao* of the Taoists, can be seen, perhaps, as the ultimate unified field, *from which spring not only the phenomena studied in physics, but all other phenomena as well.*

'In the Eastern view, the reality underlying all phenomena is beyond all forms and defies all description and specification. It is, therefore, often said to be formless, empty, or void. But this emptiness is not to be taken for mere nothingness. It is, on the contrary, the essence of all forms and the source of all life. Thus the *Upaniṣads* say (*Chāndogya Upaniṣad*, IV. 10. 4) :

> ' "*Brahman* is life. *Brahman* is joy.
> *Brahman* is the Void. . . .
> Joy, verily, that is the same as the Void.
> The Void, verily, that is the same as joy." '

Atomic physics is confronted with the problem of consciousness through the datum of the 'observer' or, to use the new, and more meaningful term coined by physicist John Wheeler, 'participator'. Accordingly, Dr. Capra says (*ibid*., p. 300) :

'In modern physics, the question of consciousness has arisen in connection with the observation of atomic phenomena. Quantum theory has made it clear that these phenomena can only be understood as links in a chain of processes, the end of which lies in the consciousness of the human observer. In the words of Eugene Wigner (*Symmetries and Reflections—Scientific Essays,* p. 172) :

'"It was not possible to formulate the laws (of quantum theory) in a fully consistent way without reference to consciousness."

'The pragmatic formulation of quantum theory used by the scientists in their work does not refer to their consciousness explicitly. Wigner and other physicists have argued, however, that the explicit inclusion of human consciousness may be an essential aspect of future theories of matter.

'Such a development would open exciting possibilities for a direct interaction between physics and Eastern mysticism. The understanding of one's consciousness and its relation to the rest of the universe is the starting point of all mystical experience. ... *If physicists really want to include the nature of human consciousness in their realm of research, a study of Eastern ideas may well provide them with stimulating new viewpoints.*'

Confirming Swami Vivekananda's view, quoted in section 22 of this lecture, that the physicist and the mystic reach the truth of unity though following different approaches, Dr. Capra says (*ibid*., p. 305) :

'In contrast to the mystic, the physicist begins his inquiry into the essential nature of things by studying the material world. Penetrating into ever deeper realms of matter, he has become aware of the essential unity of all things and events. More than that, *he has also learnt that he himself and his consciousness are an integral part of this unity.* Thus the mystic and the physicist arrive at the same conclusion; one starting from the inner realm, the other from the outer world. *The harmony between their views confirms the ancient Indian wisdom that Brahman, the ultimate reality without, is identical to Ātman, the reality within.*' (all italics not by the author).

45. Conclusion

Understood in this light, there is no conflict between science and religion, between the physical sciences and the science of spirituality. Both have the identical aim of discovering truth and helping man to grow physically, mentally, and spiritually, and achieve fulfilment. But each by itself is insufficient and helpless. They have been tried separately with unsatisfactory results. The older civilisations took guidance mostly from religion; their achievements were partial and limited. Modern civilisation relies solely on science; its achievements also have turned out to be partial and limited. The combination today of the spiritual energies of these two complementary disciplines in the life of man will produce fully integrated human beings, and thus help to evolve a complete human civilisation for which the world is ripe and waiting. This is the most outstanding contribution of Swami Vivekananda to human thought today. This synthetic vision of his finds lucid expression in a brief but comprehensive testament of his Vedāntic conviction (*Complete Works*, Vol. I, eleventh edition, p. 124 ; words in brackets not by Vivekananda) :

'Each soul is potentially divine.

'The goal (of life) is to manifest this divinity within by controlling nature, external (through physical sciences, technology, and socio-political processes) and internal (through ethical, aesthetic, and religious processes).

'Do this either by work, or worship, or psychic control, or philosophy—by one, or more, or all of these—*and be free.*

'This is the whole of religion. Doctrines, or dogmas, or rituals, or books, or temples, or forms, are but secondary details.'

This science and technique for realising the true glory of man, followed with scientific thoroughness and detachment by the sages of the Upaniṣads and revalidated by a succession of spiritual experimenters down the ages from Buddha to Ramakrishna, is glowingly revealed in one of the immortal verses of the *Śvetāśvatara Upaniṣad*, which can fittingly conclude this study of science and religion :

Śṛṇvantu viśve amṛtasya putrāḥ
ā ye dhāmāni divyāni tasthuḥ ;
Vedāhametaṁ puruṣaṁ mahāntam
ādityavarṇaṁ tamasaḥ parastāt ;
Tameva viditvā atimṛtyumeti
nānyaḥ panthā vidyate ayanāya.

The crucial subject of human freedom hangs on the slender thread of the decision between man as nothing more than a texture of cause and effect determinism like all physical nature, and man having a focus of freedom of the spirit within him. Contemporary neurological and brain research all over the world is in search of a solution to this problem. India solved this problem in her Upaniṣads long ago, from the point of view of the science of spirituality. Presenting this solution, in the light of the above verse and in the context of the contemporary discussions on the subject, Swami Vivekananda said, in the course of his historic address at the Chicago World Parliament of Religions in 1893 (*Complete Works,* Vol. I, eleventh edition, p. 11) :

'Is man a tiny boat in a tempest, raised one moment on the foamy crest of a billow and dashed down into a yawning chasm the next, a powerless, helpless wreck in an ever-raging, ever-rushing, uncompromising current of cause and effect? ... The heart sinks at the idea, yet this is the law of Nature. Is there no hope? Is there no escape?—was the cry that went up from the bottom of the heart of despair. It reached the throne of mercy, and words of hope and consolation came down and inspired a Vedic sage, and he stood up before the world and, in trumpet voice, proclaimed the glad tidings:

' "Hear, ye children of immortal bliss, even ye that reside in higher spheres! I have found the Ancient One, who is beyond all darkness, all delusion; knowing Him alone, you shall be saved from death over again."

' "Children of immortal bliss"—what a sweet, what a hopeful name! Allow me to call you, brethren, by that sweet name—heirs of immortal bliss—yea, the Hindu refuses to call you sinners. Ye are the children of God, the sharers of immortal bliss, holy and perfect beings. Ye divinities on earth—sinners! It is a sin to call a man so; it is a standing libel on human nature. Come up, O lions, and shake off the delusion that you are sheep; you are souls immortal, spirits free, blest, and eternal; ye are not matter, ye are not bodies. Matter is your servant, not you the servant of matter.

Lecture II

FAITH AND REASON*

1. Introduction

I have been asked to speak to you this evening on *Faith and Reason.* In the very peaceful, holy, and elevating environment of this ashrama, it is inspiring for the speaker and the listeners to sit together and discuss deep spiritual themes. Such an atmosphere, and this evening hour, contribute much to the lucid handling of great ideas.

I am very happy to come once again to Gwalior, this time on my way to Delhi and Srinagar, and to spend two days with you all. Already, I have completed my tour of Bangalore, Bombay, and Indore during this extensive lecture tour of our country. Everywhere, we have this kind of meetings, where hundreds of people congregate and try to understand the great spiritual and philosophical tradition of our country and its relevance in meeting the challenges of the modern

---

* Based on a speech delivered at the Ramakrishna Ashrama, Gwalior, on 26 May 1976.

age. And our subject of discussion this evening, namely, *Faith and Reason,* is very vital in this context.

2. *Conflict Between Faith and Reason: A Western Experience only, Not Indian*

In English, we call it faith and reason. In Sanskrit, there are very beautiful words to convey these same ideas. The best word for faith in Sanskrit is *śraddhā*; it is a very great word in our tradition, and conveys much more than the English word faith, or belief. The equivalent for reason in Sanskrit is *yukti, upapatti,* or even *buddhi.* How do these two, faith and reason, stand in relation to each other? So far as the West is concerned, these two have been perpetually in conflict with each other from the very beginning of history—faith in conflict with reason, or reason in conflict with faith. And most of us in India, being educated largely in the Western way, have also learnt to accept that these two are in eternal conflict with each other.

It is time that we understand the relationship between these two *from the Indian point of view.* We shall then realise that these two possess an intimate, an inseparable, relationship with each other in man's search for truth. We never experienced that recurring conflict between faith and reason which is so characteristic a feature of Western history—as much in its history of science as in its history of religion. *When we orient our minds in terms of our own tradition, we shall see not only these two, but also man's search for truth and life fulfilment, in a new light,* revealing also the complementary role of physical science and religion in the great search.

3. The Story of that Conflict in the West

Religion is based on faith ; science is based on reason ; that is how we are taught in our schools and colleges, from the point of view exclusively of Western experience. In the West, this was, and still is, true—physical science is in conflict with religion, and *vice versa.* When religion is in conflict with science, it automatically follows that faith is in conflict with reason and reason is in conflict with faith. In such a situation, it also often follows that faith is in alliance with magic and superstition, and that faith is in conflict with faith also ! This conflict between the two, and between one faith and another faith, has always been there in Western history from Greco-Roman times, and even earlier. The conflict between faith and faith, which was always there in the pre-Christian Semetic world, became intensified after the birth of Christianity, in the form of constant intolerance, violence, and war between Christians and non-Christians, on the one side, culminating in the long and bloody Crusades in the Middle Ages, and, after the Reformation in the sixteenth century, between the various denominations of Christianity itself, on the other, culminating in the devastating Thirty-years' War between Catholics and Protestants in the next century.

The conflict between science and reason, on the one side, and religion and faith, on the other, has become prominent during the last four hundred years. The West holds that reason, which is the lifeblood of science, is the deathknell of religion. That was how religions developed in the West, and its science also treated religion as outside the pale of reason. Religion became a matter of a few dogmas and creeds which you have to believe; you cannot question them, but must have implicit faith in them, and reason's role was just to justify that faith.

Such an approach cannot square with the spirit of science, which finds expression in an untrammelled search for facts and in a critical inquiry into them and a questioning of them, and in a verification of the conclusions. Thus, critical reason became the great strength of modern physical science. In the Western context, in the beginning, religion was strong, being entrenched powerfully in an established church and in its set of creed and dogma ; it had the authority to compel obedience and conformity. And it tried to suppress this new spirit of rational critical inquiry—this spirit of emerging science. But, as we have seen in recent history, after some initial setbacks, science triumphed finally ; reason rose to dominance ; and, religion based on mere faith became defeated, after being initially treated as a dangerous error but finally discarded as a harmless superstition.

4. *The Irrelevance of this Conflict in the Indian Context*

So the Western man, by the end of the nineteenth century, became rational in the name of science, superstitious, narrow, bigoted, and intolerant in the name of religion, and an uneasy mixture of both. That is the Western history which we all, in India also, were made to study and imbibe. Such an education helped us to admire the critical spirit of modern Western science, and to inspire us to apply its mood and methods to our own problems. But it also made us suspect our own ancient religion as a bundle of superstitions based on mere faith and unworthy of the modern enlightened age, and thus to reject the very spiritual foundations of our hoary culture. This encouraged a spirit of *aping modern Western approaches and ways,* and imitating its cheap and showy aspects, instead of assimilating its strong points, in some sections of our people, in uncritically and defensively returning back to our own national superstitions, in some other sections, and generally weakening our national resolve to face the challenges of the modern age in our own way, so as to ensure the historic continuity of our millennia-old national life.

At this critical juncture of our modern history, our culture produced great spiritual teachers like Sri Ramakrishna and Swami Vivekananda who taught us the uniquely Indian approach to the understanding and handling of this important problem. That approach is today teaching us in India, and all people abroad, *that this conflict between science and religion, and between reason and faith, is not a universal phenomenon, and that India's historic experience reveals the powerful presence of a philosophy and an approach that sees truth and life in its integral wholeness, and that does not allow such conflicts to arise and mar the beauty of human life and the goal of human fulfilment.* The light of that philosophy is slowly helping some of our people to realise that such conflicts are limited to Western experience only, and are not universal. *That realisation is to be achieved by all our people today.* We have to get an insight into, and a grip on, the Indian approach to the problem of the relationship between faith and reason, between religion and science.

We need plenty of science in India ; we need plenty of reason in India. But our historic experience, and our long search for knowledge and truth, tell us today that we have not to cultivate reason and science in opposition to faith and religion. Because, we did not experience or find any conflict between them, but found only kinship and complementarity. What was their relation in the Indian context ? *Every educated citizen in India today must try to get hold of that light that India sheds on this momentous problem.* Our thinking and attitude must have the impress of the background of Indian experience also, besides that of Western experience, so that we can see things in a correct perspective. It was unfortunate that, in the West, religion did not appreciate, or encourage, or accept, the spirit of critical rational inquiry, and that the West was compelled to cultivate reason and physical science as an independent and exclusive pursuit. It was unfortunate that such a development came, that so much of conflict took place, and that modern man was compelled to discard all religion while swearing by science.

Such a development produced a mood which said that, we don't want religion, we don't want to have anything to do with faith, but shall do everything through science and reason. This Western mood has unfortunately influenced millions of people in all parts of the world, and in our country too, due to the high prestige of the modern West. But, fortunately, in recent decades, the Western people themselves are not quite happy over this conflict, and are in search of a new approach and a new reconciliation.

5. *The Modern West's Recent Desire to Resolve this Conflict*

This division between the two human faculties of faith and reason has done no good to the West, except in the short run ; in the long run, it has started proving harmful to the West itself. Hence, the West is also making a reassessment of the true relationship between faith and reason. Increasing numbers of religious thinkers and institutions in the West today are seeking to find rational and scientific foundations to their religion, by putting more emphasis on experiment and experience than on creed and dogma. There are also, similarly, increasing numbers of scientists in the West who tell us today that man needs religion and faith ; not only that, they also hold that these are more important for man compared to physical science ; but they also insist that it must be a religion that can stand rational scrutiny; otherwise, it becomes mere superstition; it becomes cheap magic. It won't be true religion. *But such an approach to religion is not available to them in the West from their own historic experience. They are now in search of such an approach in the Indian and other Eastern traditions.* There is slowly growing the appreciation in the West that the Indian experience has been quite different in this field from the Western experience ; and yet, we ourselves, in India, do not know precisely what is the nature of this Indian experience, this unique Indian approach to this great subject !

The modern period of history is described as a scientific period, and science is dominated by the spirit of critical reason, questioning, investigation. It is very interesting for us to know how this new spirit appeared and developed in the modern West during the past four centuries. We are also passing through a scientific revolution in India today ; we shall be teaching science to every child in our country, from the primary school to the university level. We welcome this programme of widespread diffusion of science and the scientific spirit in our country. And it is a fact, the significance of which we should not miss to note well, that *we accord this welcome in the very light, and under the very stimulus, of our own ancient tradition,* and not in conflict with it nor to displace it, unlike what it was in the West. We and our national tradition have no fear of physical science, and of reason which is its very lifeblood. On the contrary, we welcome it, because we see something great in it. What is that something great ? As I said earlier, our national tradition recognises it in its critical spirit, in its spirit of free inquiry, in its search for truth. What a beautiful quality it is to be acquired by the human mind, and to be used by it for seeking truth and verified knowledge !

6. *The Story of the Modern West's Transition from Uncritical Authority to Critical Inquiry*

But, somehow, up to the end of the fifteenth

century, the West never felt the need for it. It was satisfied with an uncritical faith in the dogmas of its religion and with a ponderous hedged-in reason and theology to buttress that faith. This gave rise to superstition, on the one side, and to bigotry, fanaticism, violence and persecution, on the other. But, from the end of the fifteenth century, all this began to change in the West. The refreshing wind of critical reason and free inquiry began to blow, gently at first, and powerfully later, creating what is called modern science, and its fruit, the modern industrial age and the modern world. The way this spirit of science developed in the modern West is an interesting study for us in India, now that we are ourselves entering a *new* scientific age in our long history, after over five centuries of darkness of ignorance, weakness of superstition, and neglect of the physical sciences. Historians of science tell us interesting anecdotes to illustrate the onset of this critical scientific spirit in the modern West.

One such episode, which occured towards the end of the fifteenth century, has appealed to me when I first read about it. It relates to a discussion that a number of scholars had held in a library hall of the Oxford University. They were discussing what to them was a very important subject, namely, how many teeth a horse has!

They discussed it in the way they used to discuss all such subjects in those days, i.e. by referring to past authorities. They brought volumes from the library and discussed the subject in the light of what does this author say or that author say on it. And one special authority that was highly quoted and respected in those days was Aristotle. So books of Aristotle were brought out and the discussion was going on animatedly. Just at that time, the story says dramatically, one young scholar quietly left the hall. Nobody noticed his leaving. But after a few minutes, that young scholar returned to the hall, and this time nobody could fail to notice him, because *he brought in a live horse* and, stationing it in the centre of the hall, addressed his audience saying : 'Gentlemen, you want to know how many teeth a horse has ? Why go to books ? Here is a horse ; open its mouth and examine its teeth and find out the truth for yourself !'

To us of today, this act of the young scholar looks very correct and commonplace. But to the scholars of those days, it looked as a piece of irreverent audacity on the part of that young man to think that a horse had more teeth than what Aristotle had given to it, and that he should dare to ask them to independently examine its mouth !

Such episodes reveal the onset of a gentle refreshing scientific breeze in the West. That mild breeze became a powerful wind in course of time affecting the whole of Western Europe, at first, and the whole Western world, later. Today, that wind is affecting the whole world. That is the modern scientific wind, the impulse to question, inquire, and investigate nature and man, critically, freely, and fearlessly. Here is the vast world of nature ; study it, investigate it, ask questions of it, and try to understand it and get control over some of its forces, through rigorous methods *which today constitute the scientific method*. That is modern physical science, with its explosive output of knowledge—verified and verifiable, open and communicable—and the practical application of that knowledge in diverse fields of life. That is the strength of modern Western physical science and its enormous appeal to the human mind.

7. *Modern India to Continue to go after the 'Roots' of Science and not merely its Modern 'Fruits'*

Now, we want the growth of this science and this scientific method and mood in modern India. It is not enough that we go in only for the *prod-*

ucts of science, like technology, industry, labour-saving machines and gadgets, etc. We need these, but we should not be content merely with these *fruits* of modern science. We must go after, and master, that real strength of science, the very *root* of modern science, namely, pure science and its methods and results, including its conclusions about the macrocosm and the microcosm. The wonderful truths it yields to the trained human mind are abundantly illustrated in the history of modern science.

It will be very inspiring and heartening for all our children to know that, from the very beginning of our culture in Vedic times, through the Upaniṣads, Buddha, and Śaṅkara, we had encouraged this critical questioning approach to nature and man, and had developed both the physical sciences and the science of religion based on it. It is slowly being realised that ancient India made great contributions to the sciences of surgery and medicine, mathematics, metallurgy, physical cosmology, grammar, linguistics, town planning, environmental hygiene, and in other fields. We developed these physical sciences in India by the same methods which the modern West has now more thoroughly developed as the scientific method.

This can be seen particularly in the *Aṣṭādhyāyī*

of Pāṇini who lived, according to the latest research conclusions of some scholars, about the fourteenth century B.C. (about the fifth century B.C., according to earlier scholars), and who hailed from the town of Śalātura, situated near the meeting point of the Kabul River with the Indus River, in the land of the *Paṭhāns*, now in West Pakistan. Through a penetrating study of the spoken Sanskrit language of the people, the *laukika,* or the *bhāṣa,* and of the sacred *Vedic* Sanskrit, through a meticulous classification of the data collected, and through laws and rules deduced from his own and earlier investigations, Pāṇini built up, in that famous book, the science of linguistics, along with developing the philology and grammar of the Sanskrit language. No other language in the world, either before or since, has received this scientific treatment which Pāṇini, and his predecessors and two or three successors, gave to Sanskrit, and that too at so early a period of human history. He gave to each vowel or consonant a precise sound value, which made Sanskrit a truly phonetic language, and classified all the sixteen vowels and thirty five consonants beginning with *a*, the first sound produced by the throat, and pronounced as the short form of 'a' in the English word 'part', according to *sthāna,* or place of origin, *mātrā,* or duration, *abhyantara prayatna*, or internal effort, and *bāhya prayatna*, or external effort. In the words of the erudite German Sanskrit scholar of the last century. Theodor Goldstücker (*Pāṇini : His Place in Sanskrit Literature*, first Indian Edition, 1965, pp. 95-6) :

'Pāṇini's grammar is the centre of a vast and important branch of the ancient literature. No work has struck deeper roots than his in the soil of the scientific development of India. It is the standard of accuracy in speech—the grammatical basis of the *Vaidika* commentaries. It is appealed to by every scientific writer whenever he meets with a linguistic difficulty. Besides the inspired seers of the works which are the root of Hindu belief, Pāṇini is the only one among those authors of scientific works who may be looked upon as real personages, who is a *Ṛṣi* in the proper sense of the word—an author supposed to have had the foundation of his work revealed to him by a divinity.'

In his book *India as Known to Pāṇini*, Dr. V. S. Agarwala writes (pp. 2-3) :

'Pāṇini undertook a profound investigation of the spoken and the living language of his day. He applied the inductive method in discovering and creating his own material for purposes of evolving his grammatical system. As a trustworthy and competent witness of linguistic facts, he cast his net so wide that almost every kind of word in the language was brought in :

sabdāsu bahavaḥ saṁkalitāḥ, tān upādāya Pāṇininā smṛtirupanibaddha (*Kāṣikā*, IV. i. 114). ...

'On the whole, one may say that Pāṇini's grammar is related to Sanskrit like the tap-root of a tree, the source of its sap and vitality regulating its growth. For Indo-European philology, Pāṇini's work has proved of inestimable value. For Indian history and culture, the *Aṣṭādhyāyī* is a mine of trustworthy information throwing light on numerous institutions, as the present study is directed to show.'

What gifted and trained minds our ancestors had, by which they developed not only these physical sciences, but also poetry and the fine arts, and philosophy and religion! Their minds hungered for truth and beauty and goodness—*satyam, śivam, sundaram,* and possessed a passion to work for universal human welfare.

8. *The Glory of Adhyātma-vidyā*

The philosophy developed by the sages in the Upaniṣads is known as Vedānta, which they described as *Brahma-vidyā,* or *Adhyātma-vidyā,* and which they defined as *sarva-vidyā-pratiṣṭhā,* 'the basis of every *vidyā*, or science', in virtue of its vision of the changeless and non-dual pure Consciousness behind all the changeful and diverse phenomena of the world. And philosopher Gauḍapāda of the seventh century A.D., who was the guru of the guru of Śaṅkarācārya, proclaimed the glory of this unifying vision, which is wisdom, in a famous verse of his *Māṇḍūkya Kārikā* (IV. 2) :

Asparśa yogo vai nāma
sarva-sattva-sukho hitaḥ ;
Avivādo aviruddhaśca
deśitaḥ taṁ namāmyaham—

'I salute this philosophy that has taught the well-known *asparśa-yoga,* or the yoga of non-separateness, which conduces to the happiness and welfare of all-beings, and which is free from all strife of disputation and contradiction.'

There was a versatality about such a mind. It sought truth both in the outer world and in the inner world. It did not cut up its pursuit, or truth itself, into rigid compartments and say, that physical science should be pursued with the aid of critical reason and experiment, but religion should be approached simply through belief. In every branch of knowledge, whether secular or spiritual, where there is a forward thrust from the known to the unknown, there was the emphasis by these sages on *jijñāsā*, or critical inquiry. And in all such *jijñāsā*, there was a high place for faith as well as for reason. But such faith did not mean mere belief, just swallowing what was heard or said. There is a unique quality about such faith as a complementary value to critical reason.

9. *The Upaniṣads and the Critical Spirit in Religion*

From the time of the Upaniṣads, over three thousand years ago, upto our own time, we had great spiritual teachers, who were essentially great scientific investigators in the field of religion before they became its teachers. They did not present religion, therefore, as a finished creed or dogma to be swallowed without questioning, but as a subject of research, experiment, and experience.

We can see this critical inquiring spirit as a flood in the spiritual and philosophical quest of our Upaniṣads, though it is also not entirely absent in the pre-Upaniṣadic Vedic literature. The sages of the Upaniṣads dared to ask searching questions about nature, about man, and even about the tenets and gods of their inherited religion; they also dared to doubt when satisfactory answers were not forthcoming. They thereby evolved a great science of religion, not in conflict with, but complementary to, the sciences of physical nature, and also a philosophy, known later as Vedānta, unifying the physical sciences and the science of religion. Reality is one, they said, and it can be studied in its two fields of external nature and internal nature. The challenge to human search for knowledge and truth comes not only from external physical nature but also from something deep within man himself. Both these worlds are to be investigated, and both faith and reason are to be used in such investigation. We need to have faith in ourselves, in other human beings, and in the ultimate meaningfulness of the universe. Search for truth, which is often a co-operative endeavour, has no meaning without this many-sided initial faith.

10. Faith and its Role in the Pursuit of Truth

So faith becomes the very basis of rational investigation and, without faith, there can neither be high science nor high religion. Great scientists also tell us today that science needs faith, along with reason, just as our authentic spiritual teachers tell us in India that religion needs the strength of reason, along with faith. But this faith, this *śraddhā,* is different from that usual idea of faith as mere static *viśvāsa,* or belief, swallowing everything that is said by any authority without subjecting it to evidential tests. Śaṅkarācārya defines true *śraddhā* in a beautiful passage in his *Vivekacūḍāmaṇi* (verse 20) :

Śāstrasya guru-vākyasya
satya-buddhyavadhāraṇam ;
Sā śraddhā kathitā sadbhiḥ
yayā vastūpalabhyate—

'Understanding as *true* the words of the guru and the śāstra, or scripture, is called by good people as *śraddhā*, by which the *vastu*, or "the truth that already is there", is realised.'

It is faith with a view to investigating the truth of what is told ; *satya-buddhyavadhāraṇam* means 'ascertaining through reason the truth (of what is taught)'. Any fool can believe ; but that belief is to be subjected to the test of truth. That is real *śraddhā*, the capacity to convert belief into truth, and into conviction. Many modern scientists have said the same thing. Here is a luminous sentence from Thomas Huxley, collaborator of Darwin (quoted by J. Arthur Thomson in his *Introduction to Science*, p. 22) :

'The longer I live, the more obvious it is to me that the most sacred act of a man's life is to say and feel, "I believe such and such to be true". All the greatest rewards and all the heaviest penalties of existence cling about that act.'

Suppose some one says that he believes that such and such a man is dishonest; can we say that that is a true belief until it is held by him after investigating it and finding that it is true? Otherwise, it is just belief, often false belief, or prejudice. And any fool can say 'I believe' in that way; but it requires a tremendous mental discipline to be able to say 'I believe such and such a thing *is true*'. That is *śraddhā* in physical science, and that is also *śraddhā* in the science of religion. The scriptures say something, and you say that you believe it; the guru says something, and you say that you believe it. But the main question is: have you proceeded from that initial belief to the investigation of it, so that you know it for yourself to be true? That is *śraddhā*.

In the science of religion, such investigation is done by life itself, and not by mere intellectual cogitation and futile discussion. In life, it is necessary to have a few beliefs of this type of 'I believe such and such to be true', which carry creative energy with them, along with many of the other types of merely 'I believe', which are static and cozy. The former signifies *beliefs* transformed into *convictions*; and that is *śraddhā*. And '*śraddhā* is the warp and woof of man; man is man only in the measure of the *śraddhā* he possesses'—*Śraddhāmayo'yaṁ puruṣo, yo yat śraddhaḥ, sa eva saḥ*, as the *Gītā* expresses it (XVII. 3).

11. Faith and Reason Complementary

Here you can see the scientific and rational and human aspects of *śraddhā;* and all physical science, all religion, and all human life itself, needs this type of *śraddhā*. What does *śraddhā* mean in the physical sciences? It means a faith in the meaningfulness of the universe. A scientist cannot investigate into nature unless he has a prior feeling that nature is worth investigating that there is some meaning behind all the confusing mass of data before him. Without that prior faith, he cannot get even the impulse to undertake his scientific inquiry. This stimulus given by *śraddhā* is brought out by Saṅkara in another definition of the word given by him, namely, *āstikya buddhi* which, precisely translated, will mean 'the positive-attitude-oriented reason'.

Viewing faith from the point of view of scientific reason, Sir Arthur Eddington says (*The Philosophy of Physical Science*, p. 222):

> 'In the age of reason, faith yet remains supreme: for reason is one of the articles of faith.'

Says Albert Einstein in his essay on *Science and Religion* (*Out of My Later Years,* p. 26):

'Now, even though the realms of religion and science in themselves are clearly marked off from each other, nevertheless, there exist between the two strong reciprocal relationships and dependencies. Though religion may be that which determines the goal, it has, nevertheless, learned from science, in the broadest sense, what means will contribute to the attainment of the goals it has set up. But science can only be created by those who are thoroughly imbued with the aspiration towards truth and understanding. This source of feeling, however, springs from the sphere of religion. To this there also belongs the faith in the possibility that the regulations valid for the world of existence are rational, that is, comprehensible to reason. I cannot conceive of a genuine scientist without that profound faith. The situation may be expressed by an image: Science without religion is lame, religion without science is blind.'

When the *Kaṭha Upaniṣad* introduces its young boy, Nachiketā, inspired by a passion for truth and nothing but truth, it presents him as 'possessed' by *śraddhā* (1. 2) : *śraddhā āviveśa.* What does that *śraddhā* mean? Does it mean that he believed in all the cock-&-bull stories told to him by his elders? Not at all. He was in search of truth, and he had a deep faith that a profound truth lay behind the diverse phenomena of nature and life. Nachiketā's mind was thus exactly like the mind of a scientist face to face with the problem of the mystery of nature—the positive attitude of mind : *āstikya buddhi,* which is deeply convinced that there is truth hidden somewhere in the recesses of life; I am convinced of it, I am in search of it ; I have not seen it yet; but I believe it is there. Otherwise, why should I dedicate my precious young life to this arduous search, if I knew in advance that there was no truth hidden in life ?

The known world I can see and experience with my senses ; the unknown I do not see or know ; and yet I feel it is there. This basic positive attitude to the unknown dimension of reality is called *śraddhā.* No scientist can enter the field of scientific quest, much less discover any truth in that field, and no science can progress, without this positive attitude. So, in Vedānta, we emphasise the need for this *śraddhā*, the need for a positive attitude towards the meaningfulness of the world around you and in you, for this faith in your capacity to unravel that mystery, and for a sincere and sustained search in that direction. This is absolutely essential.

The opposite of *śraddhā* will make us understand better the true meaning and significance of *śraddhā*. What is the opposite of *śraddhā ?* In

Sanskrit, we call it *a-śraddhā ;* just the initial addition of *a*, to indicate the negative. In English, the attitude conveyed by this *aśraddhā,* this no-faith, in its fullest form, is expressed by a powerful word, namely, cynicism ; this cynical attitude, *aśraddhā*, is the characteristic of a cynic, one who has no faith in himself or in the world around him. His mind is afflicted with a totality of negative attitudes ; whereas *śraddhā* signifies a totality of positive attitudes, which is what Śaṅkara conveys by the term : *āstikya-buddhi.* This expresses the freshness and curiosity of a child's mind, while the other reflects the jaded and battered mind of defeated old age.

12. Faith and Reason versus Cynicism

Cynicism spells the spiritual death of man ; it scorns all values. It is the final nemesis of all civilisations rooted in a thorough-going materialism. It has afflicted, more or less, every civilisation in the past, but it has become the prevailing attitude of modern civilisation. It sets in when man is spiritually weakened through an over-emphasis on material things and organic satisfactions, and through the consequent neglect of the ever-present datum of the divine spark in man and nature. Man then loses the spiritual capacity of *digesting* experiences ; he is, on the other hand, digested by his experiences, and this results in cynicism. Many intellectuals the world over have developed this cynical attitude today ; they have lost this precious value of *śraddhā* and have become victims of its opposite, *aśraddhā.*

At no time in history has there been such a pervasive cynical attitude as we find in this modern age. Almost every intellectual is partly or wholly a cynic. And, unlike in older civilisations in which cynicism afflicted only some people in old age, and that, too, due to too much rough handling by life, in modern civilisation, it has started afflicting even children. Why ? Because, that basic *śraddhā*, which is behind all religion, behind all true science, behind all true pursuit of knowledge and excellence, is missing ; and also because, applied science has helped to sharpen modern man's craving for organic satisfactions beyond healthy levels. The intellect has become sharp and clever, it can shake or upset or destroy beliefs, of oneself or of others, but it has lost the impulse to strive for truth, or achieve goodness, or create and enjoy beauty. By seeming to know too much, and by draining away the faith in the meaningfulness of the deeper levels of life, it has dried up the springs of knowledge, abandoned all further search for truth, got stuck up at the organic level of life, and reduced life itself to boredom and frustration.

13. The Evils of Cynicism

Somebody, I think it was Oscar Wilde, has defined a cynic in one sentence, and I shall convey that to you : 'A cynic in one who knows the *price* of everything and the *value* of nothing'. He has all the information about things ; but he does not have the insight into the value of anything. Value system lies at a deeper level. To sense it, there is need for this positive attitude indicated by the word *śraddhā.* A scientist is not a cynic, he has a positive attitude. He may be a cynic in other fields of life, but not in his own field of research. The cynical attitude devalues all things of value, and drains life of all worth and meaning. To it, one's own mother is only the guy that gave birth to this body ; that's all. The cynical mind has drained away all feeling and emotion and is just logical, and assesses men and things with that cold logic.

Lokamanya Bal Gangadhar Tilak, in his famous book *Gītā Rahasya,* gives the following definition of one's mother from the point of view of such a cynical logical mind : *garbha-dhāraṇa-prasavādi strītva-sāmānyā-vacchedakā-vacchinna-vyakti-viśeṣaḥ*—'a particular individual, associated with pregnancy and delivery of children, etc. belonging to the general class of individuals limited by the characteristic of femininity.' The mother so defined cannot be recognised by any one as his or her mother ! For, all the values associated with motherliness have been drained away from it. But such is the view of things, persons, and life itself held by a cynical mind. It knows not the mother ; but it knows that it costs this much or that much to maintain that unproductive individual ! It can never understand the value system pervading and infilling particular individuals and things. This type of cold, logical, utilitarian attitude is infecting millions of people today, due to the dissociation of values, which is the gift of faith, from facts, which is the gift of intellect or reason. That is what makes reason and intellect sterile, and unfit to be the sole guide of man to truth and life fulfilment.

14. The Buddhi of Vedānta as Creative Faith-Reason

Reason and intellect become creative when faith is integrated with it. This is the *buddhi* of

Vedānta. *Buddhi* combines the creativity of *śraddhā*, with its sensitiveness to values, with the analytical power of the intellect, with its grasp of facts, and adds also the power of pure will to itself. This is *buddhi* as the integral unity of faith-reason-will, evolved by man out of the neuro-psychic energies given by nature within him, and capable of leading him not only to discoveries in science, physical or spiritual, but also to the creation of great art, and to life fulfilment itself, individual and collective.

It is thus obvious that the translation of *buddhi* as intellect severely limits its scope and meaning. Vedānta reveals its true form, when it presents it as the faculty of luminous and creative and dynamic reason. It is highly eulogised in the Upaniṣads and the *Gītā*. The *Gītā* tells man 'to put his or her life under its guidance'—*buddhau śaraṇam anviccha* (II. 49). *Buddhi* restores to the world, and to human life, the poetry and charm that was taken away by the intellect for its limited and specific handling of both. The *Kaṭha Upaniṣad* (III. 9) summons man to put the chariot of his life under the guidance, not of the chariot, i.e., his body, not of the horses, i.e., his sensory system, nor the reins, i.e., his psychic system, but of the charioteer, i.e., his *vijñāna,* i.e. *buddhi,* or 'enlightened reason'.

15. *Conflict of Reason and Faith Overcome in Spiritual Life*

Therefore, this conflict between reason and faith, between *yukti* and *śraddhā,* is overcome by the higher vision of a comprehensive spirituality of Indian philosophy. There were people in India who swore by *yukti* only, and there were other people who swore by *śraddhā* only, and they both became narrow by that isolation and specialization. We had many *paṇḍits,* or scholars, full of brain, full of what you call *yukti,* but they were warped and sterile individuals, engaged in what is termed logic-chopping, and bereft of the warmth of humanness and of a grip on the human situation arising from the culture of feelings and emotions, along with reason.

On the other hand, we had plenty of people with emotionally held beliefs, but also weak of will, with no clear grasp of facts and, often, inclined to superstition and bigotry. But our greatest teachers and books have always emphasised this harmonious combination of *śraddhā* and *yukti,* faith and reason, and also *dhṛti,* will, to emerge, as the instrument of a comprehensive spirituality encompassing the secular and the sacred, as also work and worship, as the luminous buddhi, which Śaṅkara describes as *ned-*

iṣṭhaṁ brahma, 'closest to Brahman', closest to the innermost Self of all, the ultimate Reality in man and nature, ever present just behind the human psychic system. The ordinary reason or intellect is lit only by the feeble light of the senses and the sensory world in front ; whereas, the *buddhi* is lighted by the *ekaṁ jyotiṣām jyotiḥ*—'the one light of all lights'—the Ātman or Brahman, the light of pure Consciousness.

This is the combination of *jñāna,* knowledge, *bhakti,* love of God, *dhyāna,* meditation, and *karma,* dedicated action, in the philosophy of integral yoga of the *Gītā.* The clarity and grasp of facts of the trained intellect, the emotional richness of faith, and the dynamism of will, are unified in its *yoga* of *buddhi. Śraddhā* without *yukti* is blind ; *yukti* without *śraddhā* is dry, sterile, and ineffective. That is why the *Gītā* and the *Śrīmad Bhāgavatam* lay stress on the combination of *bhakti* and *jñāna.* The latter exhorts us to practise *bhakti,* love of God, 'combined with *jñāna* and *vairāgya,* knowledge and renunciation'—*jñāna-vairāgya-yuktayā bhaktyā.* That great book is eulogised by the *Padma Purāṇa* in its *Bhāgavata-māhātmya* section thus (2. 71).

Idaṁ bhāgavataṁ nāma
purāṇaṁ brahma saṁmitam ;

Bhakti-jñāna-virāgāṇām
sthāpanāya prakāśitam—

'This *Purāṇa* is called *Bhāgavatam ;* it is based on the Vedas ; it is published for the purpose of establishing *bhakti, jñāna,* and *vairāgya.*'

It is such a *bhakti* that can penetrate into the heart of the mystery of God. Such *bhakti* and how to cultivate it, and how innumerable devotees and saints and divine incarnations have expressed it in their lives, is the central theme of the *Śrīmad Bhāgavatam ;* such bhakti is also the theme of the *Bhagavad-Gītā.*

So *jñāna* needs *śraddhā ;* and *śraddhā* needs *jñāna.* It is thus that knowledge matures into wisdom. Otherwise, that *jñāna* will be dry intellectual knowledge, and that *śraddhā* will be blind beliefs or cheap sentimentalism. Our great spiritual teachers very much warn us against that kind of one-sidedness.

If a man says, I *know* the definition of love, I have written a whole volume on it, and have got also a doctorate on that subject, and you ask him : Have you *experienced* love ?, and he replies, 'no' ; then what is the use of that voluminous knowledge ? It is better to experience love, even a little of it, than merely knowing all the learned definitions about love. Facts or data of the sensory world are to be *known* ; but values are to be *experienced.* And when so experienced, values also become facts, but of a deeper world of experience. This is why *jñāna,* if it is mere intellectual knowledge, is respected, but is not respected much. It must have some other strength behind it, namely, emotional experience. Therefore, says Kṛṣṇa in the *Gītā* (IV. 40) : *Ajñaśca aśrddadhānaśca saṁśayātmā vinaśyati*—'The ignorant man, bereft also of *śraddhā*, ever of a doubting nature, perishes.' And, after stating (IV. 38) *nahi jñānena sadṛśam*—'there is nothing equal to *jñāna,* or knowledge', Kṛṣṇa had also affirmed (IV. 39) : *śraddhāvān labhate jñānam*—'The one endowed with *śraddhā* acquires *jñānam.*' *Jñāna* backed by *śraddhā*—that *jñāna* alone is radiant and redeeming.

16. The Vital Role of Imagination in Physical Science

As I said earlier about physical science, the scientist who wants to know the truth about nature must have a basic conviction that there is truth hidden in nature. With that conviction alone can he become a discoverer of the truths of nature. Otherwise, he will remain a mere scientific scholar ; he may quote scientific opinions on various subjects ; but he cannot become a scientist himself.

The sooner we realise this truth about physical science—that pure science is the product not only of a clear reason or a sharp intellect but also of some deep faith within the scientist, faith in himself and in the truthfulness of nature—the better we shall understand the spirit of physical science and its close kinship with the other two disciplines in the pursuit of truth and human excellence, namely, art and religion, in which faith, in the form of *kalpanā,* or imagination, plays a greater role than reason.

Thus, apart from intellect or reason that functions in the discovery of truth in physical science, *imagination* also plays a vital part in all great scientific discoveries. Imagination is what helps critical reason to develop into creative intuition. In the discovery of the universal truth of gravitation by Newton, in the development of relativity and quantum theories in twentieth-century physics, in the discovery and demonstration of the unity of plants and animals, and of the living and the non-living by Sir J. C. Bose, and in several other instances, we can see this creative play of imagination, and its intuitive by-products, which are vital ingredients of *śraddhā,* or faith. Seeing a particular apple falling, Newton could make this inductive jump to the cosmic level that the same force of gravitation is what makes the moon fall towards the earth, what makes for the movements of all the planets and stars, and what reveals itself as a universal force exerted by every material body on other bodies in the universe.

Many scientists have higlighted this importance of imagination, and its fruit, intuition, as aids to critical reason, in the discovery of scientific truths. Says professor Fritjof Capra, of Berkeley University Physics department, in his fascinating very recent book : *The Tao of Physics* (p. 31) :

'Rational knowledge and rational activities certainly constitute the major part of scientific research, but are not all there is to it. The rational part of research would, in fact, be useless if it were not complemented by the intuition that gives scientists new insights and makes them creative. These insights tend to come suddenly and, characteristically, not when sitting at a desk working out the equations, but when relaxing, in the bath, during a walk in the woods, on the beach, etc. During these periods of relaxation after concentrated intellectual activity, the intuitive mind seems to take over and can produce the sudden clarifying insights which give so much joy and delight to scientific research.'

The sense organs of cognition and the sense

organs of action convert the animal body into a centre of the most dynamic and varied activity in all nature. But at the level of the senses themselves, this activity is mostly uncoordinated and automatic and, therefore, not fit for purposes beyond mere physical survival. This coordination is achieved by nature in the human body in a new faculty of, what neurologist Grey Walter calls, *imagination* (*The Living Brain*, p. 2).

It is the capacity of the organism for imaging ideas and choosing from several alternatives, before issuing forth in action in automatic response to any sensory stimulus. It is this new capacity, which even the highest apes do not possess, says Grey Walter, that gave man dominance over nature and put him on the road of a new dimension of evolution itself, in continuation of organic evolution, namely, cultural evolution ; and he adds, with a touch of humour, that, if any one doubts the power of this new image-making faculty, let him consider the consequence of any other species than man developing this capacity ; if the lion or the tiger or any other animal, for example, had developed this new faculty, we human beings would not have been here at all to discuss the subject !

Echoing the division of knowledge by ancient Indian philosophy into the sub-conscious and the unconscious, of the dream and deep sleep states, into the conscious, of the waking state, and the superconscious, of the *samādhi* state, post-war psychology suggests the addition of a third mode of cognition, called 'tertiary cognition' to the so far accepted two modes of cognition namely, the primary cognition, standing for the sub-conscious, or the pre-conscious, in which imagination has full play, and the secondary cognition, standing for the conscious, or the rational, in which the intellect has full play; this tertiary cognition combines within itself the creativity and spontaneity of the primary mode with the clarity and precision of the secondary mode.

In all these new developments of thought, we can see deeper and deeper understanding, by modern man, of the immense range and possibilities of the human mind long recognised in Indian thought. The finite mind can grasp only finite reality. The infinite reality can be realised only by the infinite mind. Purifying the mind, according to Vedānta, means eliminating its sensate limitations and its egotistic distortions. Sri Ramakrishna expresses a profound truth when he says that *śuddha manas,* or pure mind, *śuddha buddhi,* or pure reason, and *śuddha Âtman,* or pure Self, are one and the same truth.

Imagination helps reason to discover new truths by induction from the known to the unknown. A scientist starts with some knowledge and says : this much I know ; but what lies beyond it, I do not know ; but I feel it is there ; my imagination tells me that there are deeper truths beyond what I have known, and I shall continue my search for them. Here is seen the spirit of faith or *śraddhā,* which has the strength to accommodate doubt as well, doubt of the creative kind. Similarly, when we come to the world of religion, we get the intimations that there are profound truths hidden beyond this perishable world revealed by the five senses, behind this perishable psycho-physical organism, and also the fleeting ego presiding over it which I call 'myself'. We approach this profound mystery within man with the strength of this *śraddhā,* but deepened and chastened by that earlier investigation, by every human being generally and by a scientist more intensively, into the mystery of the physical universe. *Śraddhā* in religion is the basic reverential attitude that the unknown, the unseen, the imperishable exists, behind the known, the seen, the perishable. Reality as revealed by the five senses is so little ; yet it is fascinating to the human mind. How much more fascinating and rewarding must be the search and discovery of the reality that lies beyond the sensory level! All techniques of spiritual research and realisation is to proceed on the strength of this basic *śraddhā,* or faith, with its ingredient of initial creative doubt as well. Such a research will be fruitless, it is obvious, if undertaken with an initial cynical attitude and its uncreative and sterile kind of doubt.

17. 'Śraddhasva, Somya !'

In its scientifically and spiritually fascinating story, in the form of a long dialogue, of Śvetaketu's spiritual education by his father Āruṇi, the *Chāndogya Upaniṣad* highlights the need for and significance of this type of *śraddhā,* or creative faith, for man, when confronted by the mystery of the unknown behind the known.

The Upaniṣad introduces the dialogue with the story of the philosopher father sending his son, at the age of twelve, to the house of a guru for his education. The boy was returning home after his twelve-year *gurukula-vāsa,* or education 'while living in the guru's house'. The father's question to his son on his welcome home, and the son's further education by the father, have great relevance to the needed reshaping of education in our own times (VI. I. 2-3, 4-6 and 7) :

Sa ha dvādaśa varṣa upetya, caturviṁśati-varṣaḥ sarvān vedān adhītya, mahāmanā, anūcānamānī stabdha eyāya ; taṁ ha pitā uvāca : śvetaketo, yannu, somya, idaṁ mahāmanā, anūcānamānī, stabdhaḥ asi, uta tam ādeśam aprākṣyaḥ, yena aśrutaṁ śrutaṁ bhavati, amataṁ matam, avijñātaṁ vijñātaṁ ? iti.

Kathaṁ nu, bhagavaḥ, sa ādeśo bhavati ? iti—

'Going (to the teacher's house) at (the age of) twelve years, he came back when he was twenty-four years old, having studied all the Vedas, conceited, arrogant, and regarding himself as very learned ; (marking this), his father said to him thus : "O Śvetaketu, I see you conceited, arrogant, and proud of your learning, but, O amiable one, did you ask (from your teacher) for that teaching (about the one behind the many) through which what is unheard becomes heard, what is unthought of becomes thought of, what is unknown becomes known ?"

' "Of what nature, O revered one, is that teaching ?" (asked Śvetaketu).

Yathā, somya, ekena mṛt-piṇḍena sarvaṁ mṛṇmayaṁ vijñātaṁ syāt, vācārambhaṇaṁ vikāro nāmadheyaṁ, mṛttikā iti eva satyam,. . . evaṁ, somya, sa ādeśo bhavati, iti—

' "Just as, O amiable one, through (knowing) a single clod of clay all that is made of clay will become known—all forms or modifications are merely names proceeding from words, (and the knowledge) that all is clay is alone true—. . . such, (indeed) O amiable one, is that teaching."

Na vai nūnaṁ bhagavantaḥ te etat avediṣuḥ; yat hi etat avediṣyan, kathaṁ me na avakṣyan, iti; bhagavan tu eva me tat bravītu, iti. Tathā, somya, iti ha uvāca—

' "Surely, my revered teachers did not know this; for, if they had known, why should they not have told this to me? May your revered self alone tell (about) this to me." "Be it so, verily, O amiable one, said (the father)." '

Narrating the later part of the dialogue between the two, the Upaniṣad says (VI. 12. 1-2):

Nyagrodha phalam ataḥ āhara iti; idaṁ bhagava iti. Bhindhi iti; bhinnaṁ bhagava iti. Kim atra paśyasi? iti; aṇvya iva imā dhānā bhagava iti. Âsām ekaṁ bhindhi iti; bhinnā bhagava iti. Kim atra paśyasi? iti; na kiñcana bhagava iti—

' "Please bring a fruit of the yonder banyan free"; "here it is, O revered one." "Please break it"; "it is broken, O revered one." "What do you find here?" "These atom-like grains, O revered one." "Please break one of these"; "it is broken, O revered one." "What do you find here?" "Nothing whatsoever, O revered one." '

Taṁ ho'vāca; yaṁ vai, somya, etam aṇimā-

naṁ na nibhālayase, etasya vai, somya, eṣo'-ṇimnaḥ evaṁ mahān nyagrodhaḥ tiṣṭhati; śrad-dhasva, somya! iti—

'To him, he (the father) said: "O amiable one, you do not see what is, verily, this atom-like (subtle part of the seed), yet, it is, verily, by this very atom-like (subtle essence) that this large banyan tree exists; have *śraddhā* (faith), O amiable one!"'

Bringing out the profound significance of the teacher's exhortation: *śraddhasva,* at this critical and delicate stage of the investigation, Śaṅkara says in his commentary on the passage:

Sataḥ eva aṇimnaḥ sthūlaṁ nāma-rūpādi kāryaṁ jagat utpannam iti. Yadyapi nyāyāga-mābhyāṁ nirdhārito arthaḥ tathaiva iti avagam-yate, tathā api atyanta sūksmeṣu arthesu bāhya-visayā-sakta-manasaḥ svabhāva-pravṛttasya, asat-yāṁ gurutarāyāṁ śraddhāyāṁ, duravagamatvaṁ syāt, iti āha, śraddhasva iti. Śraddhāyāṁ satyāṁ, manasaḥ samādhānaṁ bubhutsite arthe bhavet, tataśca tadarthāvagatiḥ—

'It is from that which is (invisible and) atom-like and which is of the nature of *sat* (pure being), that the whole (visible) gross universe of effects, characterised by name and form etc., has come. Even though a truth established by scientific logic and scripture is accepted to be as such alone, even then, in the case of truths which are extermely subtle, there may be difficulty of comprehension, in the absence of a deeper faith, in the case of those minds that are *attached,* through natural propensities, to external sense objects ; hence said (the teacher) : "have faith". When (such) faith is present, there is the possibility of the mind calmly settling down on the truth that is sought after, in the wake of which will arise the grasp of its meaning.'

The above passages can well fit a student's approach to the comprehension of the 'field' concept in modern physics. The field is that from which particles arise and into which they disappear. It is subtle and beyond sensory experience ; and, in being no-thing, it is also everything.

To quote Professor Capra again (*ibid.,* pp. 221-23) :

'The field theories of modern physics force us to abandon the classical distinction between material particles and the Void. ... In quantum field theory, this field is seen as the basis of all particles and of their mutual interaction. ...

'The vacuum is far from empty. On the contrary, it contains an unlimited number of particles which come into being and vanish without end.

'Here, then, is the closest parallel to the Void of Eastern mysticism in modern physics. Like the Eastern Void, the 'physical vacuum'—as it is called in field theory—is not a state of mere nothingness, but contains the potentiality for all forms of the particle world. These forms, in turn, are not independent physical entities but merely transient manifestations of the underlying Void. ... The discovery of the dynamic quality of the vacuum is seen by many physicists as one of the most important findings of modern physics.'

The untrained human mind takes what is gross, and what is experienced by the five senses, as *sat*, or real, or being; and it considers what is subtle, and beyond the purview of the senses, as *asat*, or unreal, or non-being. Standing at the final precipice of thought where all being melts into non-being, human thought, whether in religion, or in physical science, in its realm of particle physics, or in its biological realm of genetics in its context of the discrimination, with respect to determining the true nature of life and of man, between what is merely the physical and chemical basis of life in the RNA and the DNA and what is life itself, needs to be fortified by creative and courageous faith to pursue truth and to recognise that very non-being as pure being, as *satyasya satyam*, Truth of truth, in the light of which all energies, physical or biological or psychical, are also realised as true, as the *Bṛhadāraṇyaka Upaniṣad* clearly expresses it (II. 1. 20):

Sa yathā ūrṇanābhiḥ tantunā uccaret,

yathā agneḥ kṣudrā visphuliṅgā
vyuccaranti ;
Evam eva asmāt ātmanaḥ sarve prāṇāḥ,
sarve lokāḥ,
sarve devāḥ, sarvāṇi bhūtāni vyuccaranti.
Tasyo'upaniṣad : satyasya satyam iti ;
prāṇā vai satyam ; teṣām eṣa satyam—

'Just as a spider (produces out of itself and) moves about in its own web, just as from a fire minute sparks fly about, exactly so, verily, from this Ātman have come forth all (physical and biophysical and psychophysical) energies, all worlds, all gods, all beings. Its upaniṣad ('mystic name') is *Truth of truth.* The energies, verily, are truth ; this (Ātman) is the Truth of those (energies).'

And the *Chāndogya Upaniṣad,* in its immediate next verse in the words of the guru-father to his son (VI. 12. 3), proclaims this *Truth of truth,* being of the nature of pure Consciousness, as the very Self of man and the Universe :

Sa ya eṣo'ṇimā, etat ātmyam idaṁ sarvaṁ, tat satyaṁ, sa ātmā, tat tvam asi, śvetaketo—.

' "This that which is the atom-like (subtle essence), this whole manifested universe has this as its self. That is the Truth ; He is the Ātman ; and That thou art, O Śvetaketu !" '

18. Reality as Akhaṇḍa Sat-Cit-Ânanda

The characterisation, in particle physics, of sub-atomic hadron reactions as a flow of energy in which particles are continually created and dissolved, and the description of the extremely short-lived hadron states as resonances, which suggest more an *event* than a material object, and which echoes the Hindu vision of the universe, at its deeper levels, as consisting of *sphoṭa,* i.e. sound, raise the question of the nature of these *events.* Modern physics has been in search of the true nature of matter. At and above the atomic level, we come across its stable atomic and molecular structural forms forming our normal physical universe of human sensory experience. Below the atomic level, physics comes across all matter in the form of energies, the description of which becomes appropriate only when done in relativistic and quantum terms which means, as remarked by Sir James Jeans, seeing nature 'after removing our human spectacles'.

As pellets of energies, the hadrons and resonances are still matter. The search for the elementary state of matter has travelled a long distance from the atoms (later designated as molecules) of early philosophers, through atoms of classical physics, to particles and the quantum field, and now to resonances, of twentieth-century physics.

It is interesting to note, from the point of view of Vedānta, that some particle physicists today raise the question, not only whether these elementary particles are really structureless and therefore truly elementary, but also whether there can be elementary particles at all in view of their participation in the interaction process which implies, in the words of Professor Capra (*ibid.*, p. 273-4) :

> 'the important conclusion that the known particles must have some internal structure, because only then can they interact with the observer and thus be detected. In the words of Geoffrey Chew, one of the principal architects of S-matrix theory, "A truly elementary particle—completely devoid of internal structure—could not be subject to any forces that would allow us to detect its structure. The mere knowledge of a particle's existence, that is to say, implies that the particle possesses internal structure." '

Vedānta finds an echo of its own conclusion in the above remark of Professor Geoffery Chew quoted by Professor Capra. Vedānta discovered ages ago that structurelessness, indivisibility, *cannot* be found as the characteristic, not only of matter and energy, including the quarks, if and when they are detected, but also of space and time, and even of the four-dimensional space-time, and that anything and everything that possess internal structure are *mithyā,* or unreal, because they are all *dṛśyam,* or *objects* of knowledge or observation, in the technical language of Vedānta, because they are also *pratikṣaṇam anyathā svabhāvaḥ*—'of a changing nature from moment to moment', as observed by Śaṅkarācārya. Vedānta, therefore, sought, in its *parā-vidyā,* or higher science, for that structureless and indivisible reality in the *dṛk,* the seer or the observer of which these are *vācārambhaṇam vikāro nāmadheyam*—'merely passing configurations possessing only separate names and forms', as expressed by the *Chāndogya Upaniṣad* quoted earlier. Vedānta discovered the *dṛk* as cit, or pure Consciousness, and as the unity of all *dṛk* and all *dṛśyam*—behind the separate and diverse phenomena of the material world outside, and all manifestations of consciousness centred in the egos of the individual *dṛks* within. It proclaimed that that pure *cit* alone is, and can be, *akhaṇḍa,* or indivisible, or truly elementary. Vedānta terms it the *akhaṇḍa sat-cit-ānanda*—the undivided Existence-Consciousness-Bliss'.

This indivisible *saccidānanda* is the *jyotiṣāṁ jyotiḥ* or 'light of all lights' ; It is the impersonal-personal God of Vedānta, both of its philosophy and of its religion. The *Jñāni,* following reason, and discrimination between the abiding and the fleeting, stresses its *nirguṇa* aspect or impersonal and formless aspect, while the *bhakta,* following *śraddhā* and *bhakti,* stresses its *saguṇa,* or personal aspect with form. This form is the condensation of the same divine ocean of Consciousness due to the cooling influence of *bhakti,* says Sri Ramakrishna. In Vedāntic *bhakti* meditation, the devotee meditates in his heart, conceived as a full blown lotus, the radiant divine form condensed out of the infinite Light of *saccidānanda,* and, later, dissolving into It at the end of meditation. *Ekam sat; viprā bahudhā vadanti*—'Truth is one; sages call it by various names', proclaims the ancient *Ṛg-Veda. Yato mat tato path*—'as many religions, so many pathways to God', proclaims Sri Ramakrishna in our own times. It is this comprehension of divine unity that made Vedānta inspire India with the vision and practice of active tolerance and harmony, not only between different religions, but also between religion and science, faith and reason, and religion and secular thought and practice. The *Śrīmad Bhāgavatam* proclaims this *tattvam,* or supreme truth, (different from *matam,* or personal preference or opinion), of all-comprehending unity in one of its famous verses (I. ii. 11) :

Vadanti tat tattva-vidaḥ
tattvaṁ yat Jñānam advayam;
Brahmeti paramātmeti
bhagavān iti śabdyate—

'Knowers of *tattvam* declare that it is one and the same non-dual pure Consciousness that is spoken of as Brahman, or the impersonal Absolute, (by the philosophers), as *Paramātman,* or the supreme Self, (by the mystics), and as *Bhagavān,* or the all-loving God, (by the *bhaktas*).

The *Jñāni* stresses the *sat* and *cit* aspects of the *tattvam* and the *bhakta* stresses these and Its *ānanda,* or bliss, aspect also in addition. It is this *ānanda* aspect that inspires all art also.

The Upaniṣads further stress this aesthetic component of the ultimate Reality by saying (*Taittirīya Upaniṣad,* II. 7. 1) :

Raso vai saḥ; rasaṁ hi eva ayaṁ labhdhvā ānandī bhavati—

'He (Brahman, as the *Bhagavān*) is, verily, *rasa* (i.e. bliss or delight) ; this (living being) experiences bliss (in life) by getting (a bit of) this *rasa.*'

The *Gītā* presents this truth of the nature of pure Consciousness, one and non-dual, and the truth of all matter and energy and all individual centres of consciousness of the universe as its configurations, in five great verses (XIII. 15-17, and 27 and 30) :

Bahirantaśca Bhūtānām
acaraṁ caram eva ca;
Sūkṣmatvāt tat avijñeyam
dūrasthaṁ cāntike ca tat—

'(It is) without and within (all) beings, both unmoving and moving; because It is subtle, It is incomprehensible; It is far as well as near'.

Avibhaktaṁ vibhakteṣu
vibhaktam iva ca sthitam;
Bhūta-bhartṛ ca tat jñeyam
grasiṣṇu prabhaviṣṇu ca—

'Itself undivided, it exists in all divided things as if divided; it should also be known as the sustainer of all things, as well as their absorber and creator'.

Jyotisāṁ api tat jyotiḥ
tamasaḥ param ucyate;
Jñānaṁ, Jñeyaṁ, Jñāna-gamyam
hṛdi sarvasya dhiṣṭhitam—

'It is the Light of all lights, beyond all darkness (of ignorance and delusion); (as the one

Self in all, It is) knowledge, object of knowledge, and the goal of knowledge, (ever) established in the heart of all'.

Samaṁ sarveṣu bhūteṣu
tiṣṭhantaṁ parameśwaram ;
Vinaśyatsu avinaśyantam
yaḥ paśyati sa paśyati—

'He sees (indeed), who sees (the one) supreme Lord existing equally (or integrally) in all beings, imperishable in things that perish'.

Yadā bhūta-pṛthag-bhāvam
ekastham anupaśyati ;
Tata eva ca vistāram
brahma saṁpadyate tadā—

'When one realises all separately existing things and beings as existing in the One, and their expansion from That (One) only, then one attains Brahman'.

Nuclear physicist Erwin Schrodinger, in his book : *What is Life* ? (pp. 90-91), echoes this Vedāntic truth of 'the unity of Âtman as pure Consciousness which is the goal of all Vedānta' —*ātmaikatva-vidyā pratipattaye sarve Vedāntāḥ ārabhyante,* as said by Śaṅkarācārya in his *Brahma-Sūtra* commentary (*Sūtra 4*) :

'Consciousness is never experienced in the plural, only in the singular. ... Consciousness is a singular of which the plural is unknown; that there *is* only one thing, and that what seems to be a plurality is merely a series of different aspects of this one thing, produced by a deception (the Indian *Māyā*).'

19. Dṛg-Dṛśya Viveka

The quantum energy field or the four-dimensional space-time, which physics presents as beyond sensory verification, finds its counterpart in Vedānta in its *Cittākāśa,* the *ākāśa* or the Void, of *citta,* or mind. This is the knowledge-field or Consciousness-field, of which the *dṛk* and the *dṛśyam* are but two poles as the knower and the known or the observer and the observed. *This Vedāntic truth will become revealed to sub-atomic physics when it resolves its present contradiction involved in viewing its 'observer' in terms of classical physics while viewing its 'observed' in terms of quantum probabilities.* Vedānta speaks of mind and matter as the subtle and gross forms of one and the same reality. Hence it was not ever obsessed, as Western thought was and still is, with the mind and body conflict or the mind and matter conflict. But, being the subtle aspect of matter, mind is not a tangible reality as matter and the physical world is.

It is about this citta or mind that the great neurologist Sir Charles Sherrington said, from the point of view of modern neurology :

'It remains without sensual confirmation, and it remains without it for ever.'

And what Sherrington said about mind is exactly what the great mathematician-physicist Eddington said about matter, from the point of view of modern physics. Eddington has also said that,

'Consciousness is the most direct thing in experience; all else is remote inference.'

This *cittākāśa* still involves the duality of the *dṛk* and the *dṛśyam*, the observer and the observed, and therefore provokes a deeper inquiry. This duality is finally overcome in the *cidākāśa*, the Void of *cit*, or pure Consciousness, which is the same *cittākāśa* viewed *non-causally*. Vedānta describes the search for, and discovery of, the true *dṛk*, or the Self, in two famous verses (*Dṛg-dṛśya-viveka*, the Discrimination between the *dṛk* and the *dṛśyam*, verses 1 and 30) :

Rūpaṁ dṛśyaṁ locanaṁ dṛk,
tat dṛśyaṁ, dṛk tu mānasam ;

Dṛśyāḥ dhī-vṛttayaḥ, sākṣi
dṛgeva, na tu dṛśyate—

'Form is *dṛśyam,* (then) the eye is the *dṛk ;* that (i.e., the eye) is the *dṛśyam,* then the mind is the *dṛk* ; the pulsations of the mind are the *dṛśyam* ; (then) the *sākṣi* or the Witness, i.e., the Self (of these), alone is the *dṛk,* (and It is always the *dṛk*) and (being self-luminous) can never be (made) a *dṛśyam.*'

Dehābhimāne galite
vijñāte paramātmani ;
Yatra yatra mano yāti
tatra tatra samādhayaḥ—

'When the notion and attachment that one is the physical body is dissolved, and the supreme Self is realised, wherever the mind goes, (there) one experiences *samādhi.*'

By thus presenting the universe, in its fundamental aspect, as pure Consciousness only, Vedānta does not *destroy* the universe or its matter but only *illumines* the true nature of both, just as modern quantum and relativity physics does not destroy the stable structures of the physical world by presenting that world as an ocean of energy only, but says that the stable familiar world presented by classical physics is only a *limiting case* of the world presented by quantum and relativity physics. Knowledge does not destory but it only illumines, says Vedānta. The material universe of daily experience, which physics sets about to study, will reveal its true form as pure Consciousness, when physics dissociates the 'matter' that it studies from the dogma of 'materialism' that it wrongly associates with it, says Vedānta. Materialism is an *intruder* in physical science while matter is a useful working concept for it, says Thomas Huxley.

The physical universe, we see and know but never experience ; consciousness, we experience but never see and know in that way. Vedānta as philosophy combines *knowledge* with *experience*. That is the meaning of Wisdom. The charge of many Western thinkers that Vedānta is no philosophy but only religion is true from this point of view ; certainly, Vedānta is not mere speculative philosophy relying only on logical reason. It emphasises the truth of the *experience* of reality, which gives Vedānta its religious character as well. Vedānta sees the limitations of that speculative reason as arising from its exclusive confinement to, and being conditioned by, the experience of the *jāgrat*, or waking state. That reveals only the not-self aspect of reality, the segment of reality studied by both Western philosophy and classical physics. But Western depth psychology and twentieth-century physics have touched a subtler dimension of reality—the self aspect, the segment revealed in the *svapna,* or the dream state. The *svapna* reveals the unity of *dṛk* and *dṛśyam* as the one *citta,* but this, not while in *svapna* when the sharp diversities of the *jāgrat* state continue to be experienced, but only on waking. And in *suṣupti,* or deep sleep state, all *dṛśyam* disappears altogether into the Void and appears again on waking. Vedānta speaks of that Void as the unity of all *dṛśyam,* of all waking and dream presentations. This is the supreme truth of the Ātman ; and this is realised in a new *jāgrat,* or waking state, called the *turīya,* or the fourth, or the transcendental.

In order to understand, to *realise,* its true nature, not merely to *speculate* about it, *man needs the strength of purest faith, along with the strength of clearest reason.* At this deeper level, faith and reason, pure religion and pure science, come together. And man needs both for the fullest comprehension of truth and for total life fulfilment. In the words of Professor Capra (*ibid.,* p. 306) :

'The modern physicist experiences the world through an extreme specialization of the rational mind; the mystic through an extreme specialization of the intutive mind. The two approaches are entirely different and involve far more than a certain view of the physical world. However, they are complementary, as we have learned to say in physics. Neither is comprehended in the other, nor can either of them be reduced to the other, but both of them are necessary, supplementing one another for a fuller understanding of the world. To paraphrase an old Chinese saying, mystics understand the roots of the Tao but not its branches; scientists understand its branches but not its roots. Science does not need mysticism and mysticism does not need science; but man needs both.'

20. *The Sruti as Âpta Vākya*

There is another consideration with regard to the validity and fruitfulness of such faith in the unseen, so far as religion is concerned. There have been, and there are, people who have gone beyond this world of the senses and discovered the Âtman, the Self, and God, the one Self of all. *Nirviklapo hyayaṁ dṛṣṭaḥ prapañcopaśamo advayaḥ*—'this *nirvikalpa,* or the transcendental, has been realised—the non-dual (reality) in which the ever-changing universe is dissolved', as the *Māṇḍūkya Kārikā* testifies (II. 35). They have realised truths which, in the terminology of

Vedānta and Buddhism, are *lokottara,* the transcendent, beyond the *loka,* or the sense-world of relativity and impermanence. And the records of these realisations are available to the rest of humanity in books like the Upaniṣads in India, and similar other books in other countries.

So, when any one proceeds on this quest, he or she has two such sources of strength behind him or her. Firstly, a general sense of the meaningfulness of the universe—that behind this organic man and his environing sensory world, there are profound truths waiting to be explored by him. And secondly, the knowledge that that *lokottara* field of experience has been already explored by hundreds of competent people, men and women, and the insights gained by them are available for the guidance of the rest of humanity. The beginner on this strange path, this challenging *terra incognita,* has something to rely upon in the insights gained by such pioneers in the spiritual path, who are truthful and trustworthy, and who also, on their part, do not ask the rest of us to blindly believe them and follow them but to use their discoveries, which are contained in the spiritual insights of the scriptures of the world religions, as starting points, and to experiment and re-check the discoveries ourselves. This is the meaning and significance of the Hindu idea of the greatness and relevance of the *śruti*, or the Upaniṣads, as *āptavākya*, words of competent persons.

About the value and limitation of all such holy books of mankind, Sri Ramakrishna humourously says in one of his parables : The Vedas, the Bible, the Koran, and other sacred books of religions *do not contain truth or God ;* they contain only *information* about truth or God. Man has to use that information to find Truth or God for himself or herself. The Hindu almanac often contains forecasts of the rainfall of the year. But if you squeeze the almanac, you will not get a drop of water ! Similarly, you will have to 'squeeze', not the scriptures, but your own experience, to get Truth, or God, concludes Sri Ramakrishna.

21. The Example of Sri Ramakrishna

This is the place of *śraddhā* in spiritual life. Sri Ramakrishna began with doubt and questioning when he started his spiritual quest as a worshipper in the Kāli temple of Dakshineswer :

'Mother, dost Thou really exist ? Books and saints say that Thou art the blissful divine energy of pure Consciousness behind the universe ; and I am here to worship Thee in this *mṛṇmayī mūrti,* or material image, and discover Thy *Cinmayī,* or pure Consciousness, form. Art Thou true ? Art Thou really the one abiding divine reality behind this changing universe ? Please reveal Thyself to me. I have heard that Thou hadst revealed Thyself to poet-saints like Rāmprasād and Kamalākānta. If so, please reveal Thyself to me also. I am just a child of Thine, with none else but Thee to guide me.'

This creative *śraddhā,* with its clear and pure imagination, fortified by an overpowering love of truth and the dynamic disciplines undergone in its search, gave to the modern world an extraordinary scientist in the world of religion in Sri Ramakrishna.

In this approach to religion by Sri Ramakrishna —and this is the authentic tradition of religion in India from the Upaniṣads, through Buddha, to modern times—we can see, in the Indian spiritual tradition, the co-existence of a luminous *śraddhā* with doubt and with a rational questing and questioning mind. His *śraddhā* did not silence doubt but quickened it and made it creative. This is also the role of doubt in all the physical sciences ; and this explains the Indian spiritual tradition's kinship with, and hospitality to, modern physical science.

22. The 'Will to Believe' versus the 'Will to Disbelieve'

Doubt based on *śraddhā* is creative; such doubt is wholesome and necessary; but mere doubt, and too much of it, is bad. If too much of 'the will to believe' is bad, too much of 'the will to doubt and disbelieve' is equally bad. Many of our modern people have this 'will to disbelieve' to an unhealthy degree, as many of our traditionalists have this 'will to believe' to an unhealthy degree. The extreme form of the former is what I referred to earlier as cynicism, as the extreme of the latter is what is described as gullibility. You tell a cynic that such and such a man is honest, he will immediately retort: Oh, I do not believe it; I have vast experience of people; I do not believe anybody can be honest! Cynicism is the tyranny of this kind of the 'will to disbelieve'; it signifies spiritual death. No such cynic can become either a physical scientist or a spiritual explorer or teacher. As a mental disease, it is more deadly than physical diseases like cholera, small pox, leprosy, and other serious ailments. It spells the death of creativity, the impoverishment of the inner man. No new truth can such a one discover, no value can such a one ever experience in life; the very impulse to seek truth and meaning has been stifled in that individual ; and this impulse to seek, and the spirit of *śraddhā* behind it, are the very life-blood of science and religion. In the words of Sir Arthur Eddington (*Science and the Unseen World*, p. 5) :

'You can neither understand the spirit of true science, nor of true religion, unless you keep seeking in the forefront.'

23. *Faith and The Parable of Fishing*

Sri Ramakrishna expounds this truth, and the meditation technique of all religions, through the illustration of fishing. What do we do when we want to catch fish ? We take a fishing rod and line, fix an attractive bait to its hook, go to a lake, and cast the line with the bait into the lake. We then sit calmly, watching. We may not have actually seen any fish in the lake, but we have the basic faith that there is fish in the lake, having heard that others have caught fish there. Sometimes, we may have to sit there for a long time. After an hour or two, if we fail to catch any fish, we won't conclude that there is no fish in the lake. We will heed the *śraddhasva somya* exhortation of the Upanisad and come again the next day and, again, the day after. We may not have caught any fish, but we continue our effort.

What is it that sustains our dogged efforts ? A basic faith that the lake does contain fish ; this basic faith is further strengthened by the knowledge that others had come before us and had succeeded in their efforts in catching fish. That means that there is fish in the lake, though we ourselves have not discovered any yet ; and that we shall also achieve success if we persist and persevere. This positive attitude, and action inspired by that attitude, are behind all discoveries of truth in physical sciences and religion.

The sages of the Upaniṣad belong to this category. Day after day, year after year, they persisted in their search for the truth of the human soul, for the truth of God. They faced all humanly impossible obstacles, disciplined their senses, calmed their minds, concentrated the energies of both and made them penetrate into the inner world, and then discovered, to their joy, and to the joy and welfare of the rest of humanity, the universal spiritual truths which have reached us through Vedānta and Buddhism.

To continue Sri Ramakrishna's parable : After long watching, we see the float trembling ; this is the visible part, from which we get the intimation about the invisible happenings below, that surely a fish is nibbling at the bait below. But soon it goes away, leaving us waiting and watching, but more strengthened in our initial *śraddhā*. And the next time, we watch the float tremble, we feel a pull at the rod and conclude that a large fish has swallowed the bait. And we pull up the line and hook, and up comes the fish into our hands ! In spiritual life, the bait that we fix to the hook of our mind is love of God and purity of character and sincerity in our search for God, which alone can attract God.

Describing this arduous technique of the pioneering sages, which yielded as its sweet fruit the pre-eminent science of spirituality, Yama the teacher tells young Nachiketā the student in a compressed verse of the *Kaṭha Upaniṣad* (IV. 1):

Parāñci khāni vyatṛṇat svayaṁbhuḥ
tasmāt parāṅ paśyati nāntarātman ;
Kaścit dhīraḥ pratyagātmānam aikṣat
āvṛtta cakṣhuḥ amṛtatvam-icchan—

'The self-existent (Reality) formed the sense organs of man with the initial defect of an outgoing disposition ; therefore, (man) sees (i.e. experiences) the external world, but not the inner Self. A certain heroic seeker turned (the energies of) his senses (and of his mind) inward, with the desire to attain immortality, and realised the (one divine) inner Self'

24. *Faith and Perseverance*

The search for truth in the physical sciences also involved similar challenges, set-backs, and disappointments, and called for similar courage and persistence to achieve final success. Behind a successful scientific discovery lie many failures and disappointments. Take the case of Madame Curie who discovered and isolated radium Behind that momentous discovery lie years and years of frustrating research with pitchblend, conducted in a damp and ill-equipped cellar, and in a spirit of what India calls *tapas,* or austere discipline in the pursuit of truth, in which she had the help and encouragement of her great scientist husband. Thus we see the close kinship in method and spirit and temper between the *tapas* and *sādhanās* of physical science and of the science of religion. Gauḍapāda refers to the dauntless persistence characteristic of all such *tapas* in a famous verse in his *Māṇḍūkya Kārikā* (III. 41) :

Utseka udadheryadvat
kuśāgreṇaika-bindunā ;
Manaso nigrahas-tadvat
bhavet aparikhedataḥ—

'The disciplining of the mind is to be pursued

with dauntless and cheerful determination just like the determination to empty the ocean, drop by drop, by the tip of a *kuśā* grass.'

The spirit behind both pure science and religion, therefore, is the same, namely, persistent search for truth ; difference is only in the field of the search. The physical scientists seek for truth in the physical universe, in the world revealed by the five senses, and by the instruments helpful to the senses. The seeker of the science of religion seeks for it in that field of experience that lies beyond that world revealed by the five senses, beyond 'where the organ of speech (and other senses), and the mind (dependent on mere sense-data), do not reach'—*yato vāco nivartante aprāpya manasā saha,* as the *Taittirīya Upanisad* puts it (II. 9). Soul and God belong to that category. That is India's testament after long experiments and verifications, from the time of the Upaniṣads to Sri Ramakrishna.

25. *The Tapas of Truth-seeking in Science and Religion*

That is why, in the field of religion in India, the question is not of believing in a creed or dogma, but experimenting with and experiencing the truth about the soul, about God. Belief is nothing. As I said in the beginning, any fool can say, 'I believe' ; and he or she believes ; yet he or she remains the same stagnant pool of a man or a woman for years and years. That belief has not made any difference in his or her character, or in his or her inter-human relationships. But one who follows the way of the science of religion does not remain satisfied with such cosy belief yielding only a static piety. He dares to question his belief, to experiment with it, and does not find satisfaction till he has converted it into a true belief. Indian history is full of accounts of spiritual seekers, drawn from all classes and levels of society, who reached such true beliefs and became saints—scientific discoverers in the field of religion. *Incidentally, it also demonstrates the truth, that the scientific mind and the spiritual mind, in a free society, can rise and flourish irrespective of caste or class or education or income levels.* They meditated and prayed, struggled and suffered, lived and worked, with dedication for years, before they experienced the light of God. The discoveries of physical science have also such *tapasyā* behind them, as the one example, out of many, of Madame Curie mentioned earlier, makes clear. *Training our children for pure science will in due course fit them for pure religion also.* Search for truth in all science begins with the sense organs, by transforming *mere seeing* into *observing.* The training of the senses and the mind into effective instruments in the search for truth and character-excellence is education ; and religion is only continued education.

26. Fundamental Science Education

The more our children get such an education, the more will trained minds be made available to our country in all fields of national activity. But, today, we are far from it ; our current education is largely *stuffing the brain* and not *training the senses and the mind.* Even in many of our university graduates, including science graduates, this power of observation is very limited, and the power of independent thinking and judgement and decision-making is still more limited. What the country needs is, therefore, not plenty of mere science graduates but batches and batches of scientific minds, out of whom will come giants in all secular and spiritual fields. That is the wonderful type of mind that can bring the galvanic touch to rouse and raise the six hundred and fifty million people of India. Quant'tatively, we are big ; but qualitatively, we are small. Our national mind is to be trained in *śraddhā,* out of which will come the creative power of imagination and the critical power of thinking.

That is fundamental science education. We need such an education to be imparted to our children from primary classes upwards. We can inspire our children with authentic stories taken from the history of physical science, for example, the story of the boy Watts who observed the power of steam and whose work later enabled Stevenson to develop the steam engine. When he was a young boy, Watts was sitting at breakfast table with the other members of his family; his mother was preparing the breakfast. The kettle, filled with water for tea, was on the fire; the water was boiling. The boy looked at the kettle; he saw the lid of the kettle jumping up; he *observed it,* not merely saw it, and felt it to be a unique phenomenon. The mother called the boy to join the party at breakfast, but he did not hear it; he was concentrated on that one single phenomenon in front of him; in the course of observation, his mind caught its significance imaginatively. There is power, or energy, hidden in the steam, it makes the lid jump up all the time, and that energy of the steam can be disciplined and made to serve the purposes of man. Out of that experience came the great discovery of the steam engine which was one of the important ingredients behind the early phase of the modern Industrial Revolution. It is this scientific curiosity and power of critical observation and love of truth, instilled in a big way in our children, that will produce the much needed scientific and social and spiritual revolution in India.

27. The Example of a Modern Indian Scientist

In one such youth of our country, the late Dr. Yellapragada Subba Row of Andhra Pradesh, we have a wonderful recent example of this scientific and spiritual quest. When I read his story a few years ago in the *American Reporter* of New Delhi (June 11, 1952), I felt deeply inspired; and I felt that we have to awaken such *Subba Row spirit*, consisting of love of truth and the inquiring spirit, and also love of man, in many thousands of our youths, before we can become a scientific nation. What did he do? As a student at school at Madras, he was a bright boy, but very poor. His brother fell ill of sprue of a serious kind. The boy watched his brother sinking day by day from what, at that time, was an incurable malady. Helplessly watching his dear brother dying away, his imagination became fired with the thought: Why is my brother dying like this?

Is there no remedy for this serious ailment? And he, then and there, resolved within himself that he would dedicate his life to find such a remedy. That is the confluence of *tapas* and *svādhyāya*, self-discipline and study-research, pursued by him thereafter till his own death—a confluence highly praised and prized in *Vālmīki Rāmāyaṇa* and other great books of Indian culture.

What a resolution for a young and poor school boy to take! But, when behind such resolutions lie love of truth and love of man, and courage, they cease to be idle resolutions of immature minds, but become silent onward creative movements of the human soul. Love of truth and love of man go together in many scientific and spiritual discoveries, and also in many social undertakings like prison reform. All antiseptic measures in modern surgery, and penicillin among drugs, are a few of the many such scientific examples. Buddha's compassion for man made him discover profound spiritual truths during his historic meditation under the *bodhi* tree at Buddha Gaya two thousand five hundred years ago. Gandhiji's going to prison, armed with truth and non-violence only, was with a view to releasing millions of his countrymen from the larger prison of political slavery and helplessness.

After his matriculation, young Subba Row was

helped by friends to study medicine. He finished duly the M.B.B.S. and M.S. courses. But, all through, only that one idea dominated his mind : how to discover a remedy for that pernicious ailment ? So, after finishing his medical course at Madras, he wanted to do research. But where were such research facilities in India then ? So he went first to U.K. in 1923 and then to America where he joined a research team at the Harvard University. Along with doing commendable research work there, he also worked hard and obtained a degree in biochemistry. During this time, he did also menial jobs to earn money to meet his expenses. He later accepted an invitation extended by the Lederle Laboratories of the American Cyanimid Company, New York, in 1940, to use its facilities for his research. Impressed with his earnestness and talents, the management of that drug-research laboratory encouraged him to go ahead in his search and, from 1942, to direct the research work of its team of scientists.

Research with tons of liver for experiment continued for years. Like many other scientific seekers, he also must have often experienced frustration and dejection for not getting the expected results. Ultimately, he succeeded in isolating a tiny bit of folic acid, and, later, his team succeeded in producing synthetic folic acid in the form of a yellow powder in 1945. It was a great discovery. Then came its testing by application to hospital patients. When it was administered, the results were marvellous, and it soon entered the market as a wonderful remedy for this pernicious disease.

He did not take any personal credit for this discovery, but he gave that credit to the members of his team. Soon after, he and his team developed another wonder-drug, aureomycin. During all those years, he gave freely from his earnings to relieve the sufferings of other people around him. Dr. Yellapragada Subba Row died young in 1948 at the age of 52 in the United States, after ensuring, through his work, life for millions of his fellow human beings.

The Lederle Laboratories have honoured his memory with the installation of his bust in their laboratory at Bulsar, Gujarat state, below which is a description of him as scientist, teacher, philosopher, humanitarian, followed by the inscription : *Science simply prolongs life ; religion deepens it.*

His life illustrates the spirit conveyed in a brief but powerful utterance by queen-mother Vidula to her prince-son Sañjaya, as recorded in the *Udyogaparva* of the *Mahābhārata* (120. 15) :

Muhūrtaṁ jvalitaṁ śreyo
na tu dhūmāyitaṁ ciram—

'It is better to flame forth for one instant than to smoke away for ages !'

I have given this example of young Subba Row to emphasise that pure science needs, along with critical reason, tremendous *śraddhā,* with its richness of imagination, out of which comes not only science but also humanism. And, in religion, we have this fund of imagination in our *bhakti* tradition, and this kind of critical reason in our *jñāna* tradition.

28. *The Ancient Example of Hanumān*

Jñāna is meant to discipline faith and imagination so that all three issue forth as a socially-oriented will towards dedicated and heroic action. This is the comprehensive spirituality of the *buddhi yoga* of the *Gītā.*

One of the finest examples of this comprehensive yoga in our national spiritual tradition is Hanumān. He was at once a *bhakta,* rich in emotion, and a *jñāni*, *buddhimatāṁ variṣṭham*—'the greatest among men of *buddhi,* or reason', as our *Rāma-nāma* hymns put it. So, on the one side is *bhakti,* based on emotion, imagination, and feeling; on the other side is *jñāna,* based on reason and discrimination. And both found expression in him in heroic action and the strong dedicated will behind it. As taught by the *Bhagavad-Gītā,* the true *bhakta* is he who combines within himself clear thinking, rich emotion and imagination, and strong will. That is the profound teaching of the *Sanātana Dharma,* or Eternal Religion, of India. Any and every foolish belief and superstition is not part of religion; believing in all sorts of cock-&-bull legends and stories, which have no human reference or moral and spiritual appeal, is not part of religion; believing in cheap magic and miracles is no part of religion.

Religion is a profound discipline of the human mind in search of the immortal and the divine, through the penetration of the outer sensory crust of reality. We achieve this, in its early stages, through the discipline of the physical sciences and through the ego-expanding ethics of socio-political discipline, making for progress in man's psycho-social evolution with its character-fruits of love, dedication, and service. But the highest truth, which lies at the deepest level, is obtained only in the experimental dimension of religion, in the higher field of the science of spirituality. And, being the birthright of all, this truth is realised within man himself as the infinite eternal Âtman, which is realised also outside as the infinite Brahman, the one Self in all nature and man.

29. *The Methods and Fruits of Inner Penetration*

How can these eyes show it, how can these ears manifest it? None of the sense organs, nor the mind in captivity to the sense organs, can reveal it. But the mind that has become pure, that has become concentrated, that has unified within itself pure imagination, pure intelligence, and pure will, becomes *buddhi*; and this *buddhi* can penetrate into the heart of this truth. As expounded by Yama to Naciketā in the *Kaṭha Upaniṣad* (VI. 7-9):

Indriyebhyaḥ paraṁ mano
manasaḥ sattvam-uttamam ;
Sattvād-adhi mahān ātmā
mahato'vyaktam-uttamam—

'Superior to the sense-organs is *manas* (mind); more excellent than *manas* is *buddhi* (reason); higher than *buddhi* is *mahat* (the cosmic mind); higher than *mahat* is *avyakta* (nature in its undifferentiated state).'

Avyaktāt tu paraḥ puruṣo
vyāpako'liṅga eva ca ;
Yaṁ jñātvā mucyate jantuḥ
amṛtatvaṁ ca gacchati—

'Superior even to *avyakta* is the *Puruṣa* (the Self), all-pervading and entirely devoid of any particularising indicative mark, knowing Whom every *creaturely* man is emancipated and attains immortality.'

Na saṁdṛśe tiṣṭhati rūpam-asya
na cakṣuṣā paśyati kaścanainam ;
Hṛdā manīṣā manasā abhiklṛpto
ya etat viduḥ amṛtās-te bhavanti—

'His form is not within the field of sight, none can see Him with the (physical) eye ; He is revealed in (the Void of) the heart by the *manas* that is fully under the control of the *buddhi*. Those who realise this become immortal.'

You cut open the physical body and examine it. Can you see the Ātman there ? Not at all ; for it is the Self and not the non-Self ; it is the *dṛk*, the seer, the observer, and not the *dṛśyam*, the seen, the observed ; and *physical* science has no relevance there ; its work will end, in its field of pure science, when it lands the human seeker on the shores of the unknown *dṛk* at the end of its voyage of discovery of the world of the *dṛśyam*. The Âtman is seen, says the last verse, by a penetrating vision, which is the product of a converging life-endeavour based on moral character and the concentration, and the turning inward, of the energies of the senses and the mind.

Indian tradition emphasises that the *Śruti* (the Upaniṣads), has no authority in the sensate field of experience. There we have to follow the authority of the physical sciences. So when our body is sick, we are to take help of the physical science of medicine, which may be modern allopathy, or yoga-aided psychiatry, or homeopathy, or ancient *āyurveda,* or nature cure. It will be foolish to go to quacks and religious magicians to get a cure. But when the ailments are spiritual, arising from what the Hindu tradition characterises as the *ṣaḍ-ripus,* or 'six enemies', namely *kāma,* or lust, *krodha,* or anger, *lobha,* or greed, *moha,* or delusion, *mada,* or pride, and *mātsarya,* or violence and conflict, it is advisable to turn to the science of spirituality for help. For the production of physical food and clothing and shelter, man has to resort to the physical sciences. But, for the production of love and kindness, compassion and dedication, peace and fulfilment, man has to resort to the science of the inner life which is religion.

In the field of physical science, we depend on the sense organs and the information supplied by them. But in the field of the science of religion, we say good-bye to the sense organs, and to the sensate mind, and to the world revealed by them. Meditation is the unique technique of the science of spirituality. The first thing we do in it is to take leave of the sense organs and the sensate mind. They are of no use to us there. Because, we are not then in search of the reality revealed by the sense organs. If that reality alone existed, there is no meaning in our closing our eyes or other sense organs, and calming our minds. We should rather keep them wide open and scatter their energies outside, which is what we do in our so-called 'normal' worldly life. But we feel that a deeper, vaster, and more meaningful dimension of reality, and of our own personality, waits for us above the sensate level. And to come in touch with it, we feel the need to discipline the senses and to calm the mind, two processes known as *dama* and *śama* in the Hindu tradition, which is the mental counterpart of the physical homeostasis achieved by nature for us in the long course of organic evolution.

That modern physical science is on the brink of a similar productive confrontation with the new datum of mind and consciousness is evident in nuclear physics itself. Twentieth-century biology presents it, similarly, in its stress on organic evolution rising, at the human stage, to the higher level of psycho-social evolution. Other scientific writers of the post-war years also refer to this exciting possibility. One of such is contained in an article on 'Aspects of an Upheaval in Medicine' by H. Schipperges appearing in Sieman's *Electromedica* journal, 5/1970 issue. It says (p. 300) :

> 'Scarcely have we discovered the cosmos and are behind the moon, when there awaits us a new universe, namely, the full inside of nature, the kingdom of the "Soul", as it was previously called, the dimension of depth, that "in the inside there is also a universe" as Goethe said, actually a multiverse, the perspective of our modern world which nowhere shows *the* world but worlds, situations, anthropologies, fragments, aspects in upheaval. Everything in this grandiose, hectic, and also moving panorama of the ending second millennium points to the conclusion that we are in the middle of a second enlightenment.'

Sir Charles Sherrington had pointed out, as referred to earlier, to this mystery of mind and consciousness, haunting his subject of neurology, during his Gifford Lectures on *Man on His Nature* (p. 266, Penguin edition, 1951) :

'Mind, for anything perception can compass, goes therefore in our special world more ghostly than a ghost. Invisible, intangible, it is a thing not even of outline ; it is not a "thing". It remains without sensual confirmation, and it remains without it for ever.'

It will be interesting to read, side by side of this, what Sir Arthur Eddington said, as referred to earlier, about the equal mystery of 'matter' in the introduction to his Gifford Lectures on *The Nature of the Physical World* :

'In the world of physics, we watch a shadowgraph performance of the drama of familiar life. The shadow of my elbow rests on the shadow table as the shadow ink flows over the shadow paper. ... The frank realisation that physical science is concerned with a world of shadows is one of the most significant of recent advances.'

30. Static Piety versus Dynamic Spirituality

In the light of such inner penetration achieved by Vedānta. India's testament is that, whether it is physical science or the science of religion, *śraddhā,* or faith and *yukti,* or reason, need to co-operate with each other, and that they never conflict with each other, if the search is for truth and human fulfilment. The more you strengthen your reason, the better for your religious life. Any foolish and fitful imagination, any foolish and temporary emotion, is not *bhakti*. *Bhakti* is that emotion directed towards the object of *bhakti*, namely, God Himself, who is of the nature of infinite love. Sri Ramakrishna said : be a *bhakta* but don't be a *boka* ! In Bengali, *boka* means a fool. Our country has too many *bokas* passing as *bhaktas,* for want of the strength of knowledge, or *jñāna,* and reason, or *yukti*. It is such *bhaktas* that are cheated by pretentious gurus and miracle mongers. A true *bhakta* cannot be cheated by anybody. But, unfortunately, I find, in our country, many *bhaktas* becoming easy prey to such imposters. They are predisposed to be thus cheated because they have dispensed with all knowledge and reason in their religious life. They are not interested in truth, but only in a little sentimentality, or in some religious sensationalism. When our people understand religion correctly, that it is a science and, as a science, it is based on both reason and faith, just like any physical science, we shall see the flowering, more and more, in our country, of true religion as *dynamic spirituality,* and the withering away, more and more, of the current noisy, showy, and *static piety,* or piety-fringed worldliness, mistaken as religion by many people.

31. Faith and Reason versus Miracle-mongering

The science of religion, based on faith and reason and experience, cannot thrive so long as people run after magic and miracles, so long as they cannot discriminate between a magic mango and a real mango. *To associate magic with religion is to vulgarise religion, to kill religion.* Modern physical science, also based on faith and reason and fact, developed only when it became dis-associated from magic. The same is true with the science of religion. The true 'magic' and 'miracle' of the science of religion is character-strength, fearlessness, peace, love, service, and dedication, just as the true 'magic' and 'miracle' of physical science is clear thinking, all-round enhancement of the physical and social welfare of man, and technical marvels.

The great spiritual teachers of India were, like modern physical scientists, teachers of verified and verifiable truths. These are what we get from the Upaniṣads, the *Gītā,* and from the books relating to teachers like Buddha, Sri Ramakrishna, and Swami Vivekananda.

In fact, one great utterance of Buddha, which I wish to repeat before every audience in India or abroad, is the exhortation to rationally examine a teaching before believing in it. It is known in Buddhist literature as *Address to the Kālāmās*. On the subject of secrecy also, Buddha has said something which I wish all students in India will keep in mind, both students of science and students of religion, so that we shall have a total scientific revolution in this country, both in the outer physical world and in the inner spiritual world. Addressing Ânanda, Buddha said : Secrecy does not belong to the *Tathāgata* (Buddha). Buddha's teaching was open ; it was *ehi passa, ehi passa*—'come and see, come and see', as he himself described it. Buddha added : Secrecy belongs to three things, O Ānanda ; What are they ? Secrecy belongs to priestly knowledge, to false doctrines, and to prostitutes ! These are Buddha's weighty words. If our people will assimilate the spirit of these two utterances of Buddha, we shall witness the flowering of true religion and true physical science in India.

32. *Conclusion*

The scientific temper and attitude, with its passion for truth and stress on verification of conclusions, is thus common training for religion and for physical science, as understood in

Vedānta. A scientist discovers some truth in his laboratory ; he publishes it in a scientific journal. Another scientist checks it up and verifies it. Still it is not enough. Several other research workers re-check it. And it finally emerges as an established scientific truth. So also was the process in the world of religion in our Upaniṣads. A sage discovered the divine core in man behind his physical, neural, and psychical dimensions ; and he called it the Âtman, the divine Self. Another sage took up this challenging conclusion and re-checked it and found it as true ; then it passed the test of several other sages as well. And, finally, it emerged as the truth about man, as the truth of the science of human possibilities, proclaiming the infinite dimension of what, to the senses, appears as the finite organically limited man. This is not, therefore, a mere opinion or personal view ; it is the deepest truth about man, about all men. And any one can re-discover it for himself or herself. It is *vastu-tantra-jñāna*—'knowledge based on the *vastu,* or existing fact, or truth', as described by Śaṅkarācārya in his *Brahma-Sūtra* commentary.

Hence its message is : *vedāhametam*—'I have realised it' ; I have known it, not that *I just believe in it ;* and *all else can also realise it.* Note the language when a verified and verifiable truth is what is being communicated. From those ancient sages of the Upaniṣads over three thousand years ago, to Sri Ramakrishna, in our own time, this is the authentic temper and language of Indian spirituality, which explains its continued vitality and its appreciation and comprehension of, and welcome to, the critical rational temper and approach of all physical science, ancient and modern.

INDEX

*** ***